To JOHN & AUDREY
with [?]

CW01080501

21

LOOKING
FOR
TROUBLE

Life and Times of David Tindall,
Journalist and Broadcaster

Cover illustration by the author
Painting of the author on the back cover by Helen Margaret

For Rowena and Gerry, our children and grandchildren

Looking for Trouble
Published 2021 by David Tindall
Email: david.tindall2019@gmail.com

Typeset by John Owen Smith
v2

Printed by KDP

Contents

Illustrations

CHAPTER 1

BOYHOOD AND THE BLITZ

The sounds, sights and smells of life in Second World War Britain linger in the memory forever, waiting to be evoked, clear as yesterday: the wail of an air-raid siren, the bee-like drone of Heinkel bomber squadrons coming in for the kill, screaming shells and paraffin heaters warming our nights spent hiding in a dank shelter below ground. Holes and rubble where houses had stood the day before and the German propaganda machine breaking into our air waves daily with Lord Haw-Haw, threatening death and destruction. Our budgerigar's shrill response every time he heard the word Germany on the radio: Stuff Hitler...Stuff Hitler. The BBC Home Service, the Radio 4 of its time, trying its best to put a smile on our faces with shows like ITMA, It's That Man Again, headed by its star comedian Tommy Handley who had a German character called Funf, being relentlessly debunked by the gag writers.

'Hello, this is Funk speaking...'

Tommy Handley: 'it may be funf to you mate, but it's not much funf for me.'

Britain's limited television service had been suspended for the duration of WWII and so radio was our main source of information and entertainment. We had the Radio Doctor telling us how to deal with common ailments and detailing symptoms of serious diseases to watch out for, diphtheria, polio and scarlet fever being the most common at the time. We had The Kitchen Front, telling us what kind of meals we might cook with the meagre rations available.

Everyone tuned into the daily news bulletins which kept us abreast of what was happening with our armed services. The main radio newsreaders, Alvar Lidell and Freddie Grisewood became almost family friends.

There were memorable war reports from John Snagge on the fall of France to the Germans and later on the D-Day landings; Frank Gillard, Wynford Vaughan Thomas and Richard Dimbleby gave us the first horrific eye-witness accounts when concentration camps like Bergen-Belsen were liberated, later in the war. Like so many people in Britain at that time, I was brought up on this daily diet of news from the front line.

I was born in Wakefield in the West Riding of Yorkshire on 13th December, 1934 but I was brought up in Manchester, where my father, Reg, had gone in search of work during the 1926 General Strike. He joined the Manchester City Police Force and had risen to the rank of inspector by the time of the declaration of war in 1939. He was based in the city centre's A Division, where he made a number of friends who were reporters on the national newspapers, all of which printed in Manchester. It was through them that my fascination with journalism was later to blossom.

After war was declared, my father started German lessons with an old friend Nora Ziegler and had acquired a working knowledge of the language by the time he joined the army. Voluntarily or conscripted, I am not sure.

When the bombing of British industrial cities started in 1940, the German Luftwaffe would try to soften us up with a cynical system of double raids: first dropping showers of incendiaries to set fire to buildings thus lighting their way, followed by another attack with high explosives. The particular drone of some four hundred Heinkel bombers was etched on our minds, presaging the rising pitch of the sirens warning us to dash for cover, which in my case was the Anderson air-raid shelter dug into our back garden. Even eight feet below ground the blasts would shake sand down on us from the bags on our corrugated iron roof, but these lonely, nerve-racking, nights were lightened by the periodic arrival of our guardian angel, Doris, the woman in black, our air-raid warden-cum-ambulance driver, who, so far as I was concerned was the bravest person I'd ever known, dashing about helping people through the thick of it all.

Doris was our hero. Each evening, when she went on duty she would put on make-up as though she was going out for a night on the town: bright red lipstick, rouge on her cheeks and silk stockings made from captured German parachutes which were apparently of very high quality: good for making French knickers too, or so my mother said. Doris was a tall, slender woman, always with a cheery smile, appearing at our shelter several times during the night, sometimes with sandwiches and flasks of cocoa. She would calmly reassure us that all would be well by the morning and then off she would go again into the night … a dashing figure in her black beret and black ankle-length coat with its red cross on one arm. With the dawn came the sound of the 'all clear' and we, my mother if she was there, my sister Hilary who was only a toddler and myself would emerge to discover what was left of our little world. Before long there would be Doris again, magically unscathed by her night's work, giving us all a hug.

We were lucky. Not all families had time to build a shelter before the air-raids on Manchester began. At this point in 1940, the country had a shortage of fighter planes: Britain's defence system largely consisted of anti-aircraft guns and searchlights. The Government, led by Winston Churchill, had also introduced food rationing and there were queues for everything. Though we were not told at the time, there was a point when the nation had only three weeks supply of food left as a result of the success of the German campaign using wolf-packs of U-boats to attack the Atlantic cargo ships heading for England, mostly coming from America.

Many of the factories around us in Manchester had turned to making munitions for the war effort. All the railings outside houses had been ripped out to be melted down and made into bullets. All gardens were churned up to grow vegetables. People started rearing chickens for their eggs and meat, and I learned how to make a snare to catch wild rabbits. One day a supply ship had got through the U-boat stranglehold on England and somebody brought a banana to my primary school, something we had never seen before. We crowded round a boy clutching this odd fruit with its blackened skin. These days one look at a banana like that and it would be immediately thrown in the bin, but we all reached out to grab a bit of it and in seconds the whole thing had disappeared down our throats, slimy skin and all. So much for bananas.

At my little school, Ladybarn Primary in Manchester, the wartime food was far from interesting; but I had heard that a Catholic school a short walk away laid on fantastic stews. So one day I decided to pay them a visit. I just sat down amongst other boys in their canteen and when our table was called, I went along for ladles full of juicy beef stew and mashed potatoes. It seemed really quite delicious. None of the teachers took any notice of the stranger in their midst, so I reckoned it was probably OK to eat anywhere I fancied.

For a few weeks I carried on enjoying the wholesome Catholic grub, until one of the teachers at my school, who had finally noticed I was absent at meal times, asked my mother if I had decided to walk home for lunch. She apparently explained that I didn't seem to care too much for boundaries in life, thus far, so the best thing to do when I came back into the classroom would be to ask me outright where had I been for lunch? The teacher, Miss Holbrook, did just that and I immediately launched into lavish praise of the beef stews at St. Joseph's down the road. Some of the children giggled and the teacher formally informed me and the rest of the class that popping into other schools to eat their food whenever one felt like it, was forbidden.

In those days, whenever I wasn't at school or during holidays, I was allowed out to play wherever I liked, so long as I was back before dark. It was the same with all my friends. A favourite spot was on open moorland, among the heather, with its steep dips and hollows and rivulets tumbling through the crags. It was also a favourite place for gypsies to park their old-fashioned caravans. My grandmother warned me to be 'careful up there, you might get carried off.'

Sometimes we would explore a more civilised urban park with tennis courts but that was nowhere near enough fun. For a start, none of us played tennis or had ever thought about it. It was as though the people who played that game were of a different species. They looked different in their smart new sports-gear and strutted about with a confident air of superiority, which suggested to us that they must have a lot of money. They were definitely posh. Tennis would never be the game for us, although my uncle Bob, in Wakefield, had found himself a girlfriend who actually played tennis: so she was definitely posh. She always wore nice clothes and lived in a three-bedroomed semi with proper curtains. When she went to the tennis courts with all her fancy stuff, she looked like a film star.

One August, when the grass in the local park was high and bone dry, our gang built a little campfire in an out of the way corner but the wind fanned the flames and the fire was quickly out of control, sweeping across a huge area of parkland like an inferno, smoke obliterating the tennis courts. We ran for cover in some bushes. We were really scared. In no time there were police cars and fire engines soaking the entire area with people being cleared from the park. Later, with pictures of it all in the local paper, my mother started to ask questions about where we'd been that day.

Somehow she seemed to know that we might have had something to do with it and kept on at us relentlessly, until finally I told her what had happened. 'How would it look...policeman's son wipes a park off the map!' I pleaded with her not to tell anyone but she made me pack a few things into a little bag saying, 'this is the last straw. You are nothing but trouble; I'm sending you to Borstal.' These detention centres were for seriously delinquent youngsters. I had heard about them many times, though naturally I didn't think I was deserving of such harsh treatment.

It was early evening when my mother marched me off with my bag to a grim-looking Victorian building, not far from where we lived. I couldn't see any sign that it was a Borstal, but it looked frightening enough: my mind was running wild with thoughts of what it was going to be like for me inside. She stopped outside, silently waiting for someone to open the gates. It seemed like an age before she finally spoke: 'I'm going to give you one last chance'... and with that she swept me off to the pictures.

Life seemed to be so full of obstacles to overcome. I had been having trouble with my private music teacher, a Miss Heales, who charged a shilling per lesson. I had decided that paying money to learn how to play the piano was a waste of time, so I pocketed the shilling and went to the cinema. I then forged my father's signature on a letter to the music teacher, informing her that 'because my son appears to be making such little progress', he was stopping the lessons.

Later, my father ran into Miss Heales in the street and the truth came out. That boy is always looking for trouble. He was absolutely furious and determined that I would learn to play, whether I liked it or not. He enrolled me in the prestigious Manchester School of Music, under a Professor Viney, a very strict lady from Eastern Europe and for several years I was imprisoned with her every Saturday morning, until she felt that I was ready to take part in a concert at the Free Trade Hall in Manchester. Thanks to her, I do know my way up and down the keyboard.

Myself tickling the ivories in later life

My mother was pleased about the lessons because at least she knew where I was on a Saturday morning and I could also now play some of her favourite songs, well enough for a good old sing-song around the piano. More importantly, I learned to play Boogie-Woogie. At this time I was madly in love with a girl in our street called Barbara Walton. She was older than me and I knew she liked that sort of music. She was at a neighbourhood party one evening and my mother, who knew that I fancied Barbara, told me to get on the piano … tickle the ivories. I launched into a few Winifred Atwell numbers and everyone took to the floor jitterbugging. I could see the girl was pleasantly surprised and I mentally I chalked up a point in my favour.

CHAPTER 2

THE EVACUEE

Before we acquired our own air-raid shelter, children at my primary school were evacuated to the countryside, in my case to Poynton, a village in Cheshire. By the time we got there by steam train, gas masks slung round our necks, I was in a pretty grubby state and had no idea of what was going on, as we were assembled in the village hall to meet local volunteers who had each come to pick up a child to take home. As the numbers thinned out, it dawned on another boy and on myself, both of us about seven, that this was some kind of selection process: it didn't seem as though anyone was interested in either of us. Even when everyone had gone and we were left on our own with a janitor we weren't at all worried. If these people didn't like the look of us, we didn't like the look of them and so we ended up spending the night on camp beds behind some curtains in a corner of the village hall.

The janitor gave us each a shilling to go out and buy fish and chips and with that we were more than happy. I remember we had to stand on tip-toe to reach the very high counter in the shop. The next day a kind lady came into the village hall and said she would take both of us, but it didn't last long. She had no spare beds, so tried to accommodate us on the floor of her sitting room. The poor lady wasn't used to dealing with young boys and did not take kindly to the mess we had created overnight. After breakfast she took us back to the village hall and handed us over to the janitor. We stayed there a few more nights behind the curtains on our camp beds and then our mothers, having heard we weren't too popular, came to collect us. While I had been away, my mother had persuaded the fire brigade to provide us with an air-raid shelter.

At first it was exciting being woken in the night to the sound of the siren wailing and having to make a dash for it. The worst bit was waking up sometimes to find that my mother was not in the house. My sister Hilary, then only three or four years old and I were alone. I hated that. Fortunately, Hilary and I had plenty of practice runs to time ourselves between our bedroom and the shelter in the garden, so turned it into a bit of a game. That way she wouldn't cry when we did it for real. But I felt very much alone, even though I tucked myself up with Hilary.

There were times when my nerve cracked during an air-raid and I would rush across the road carrying Hilary to Mrs Moore, a kindly neighbour. She kept asking me where our mother was and all I could say was that she was out with friends and had probably got stuck there when the siren sounded. Of course I loved my mother and didn't want to get her in trouble with the neighbours for having left us alone. She was usually back pretty quickly though, once the air-raid was over, but with my father away in the army I actually wondered if she had a boyfriend.

I suspected rightly, for one Christmas, when I had come into the kitchen from chopping wood I found him kissing her, so I threw the axe at him. The blunt end caught a good blow on the side of his head and it bled. I never saw him again after that, but I was always worried that my parents might split up and then where would we be?

I developed a nervous tick, a twitch, so when my father came home on leave he took me with my mother to see our GP, a Dr. Savage, who asked them if there were any problems at home. My mother just blamed everything on the war. I was on the brink of telling them all about my mother's behaviour, but I did not want to make things more difficult for her, so I said nothing. Before he went away again my father had said, 'you're the man of the house now, so look after your mother.' I was only seven, but I did feel very protective of her and she didn't bring any more boyfriends back to the house.

During the raids we were lucky to have Doris, our heroic air-raid warden, dropping in to make sure Hilary and I were alright. After a few weeks of the nightly ritual with disturbed sleep, as bombs exploded in the district, we children became over-tired and irritable and although we could see for ourselves the damage caused in the raids, there was still the excitement of collecting shrapnel in the street the next morning to take to school.

The boys had started a competition to see who could find the most interesting bomb fragments. At that age we didn't make the connection between these beautifully coloured pieces of grey metal and death. There were bright streaks of red and violet, green and blue and the edges were hideously sharp. Any one of these pieces flying through the air could take your head off. A prize 'find' would be the intact tail fin of an incendiary bomb, partly buried in the earth, until Doris warned us that some of these might be extremely dangerous and might not have gone off, so needing to be detonated by the army's bomb disposal team.

Myself, aged six, as an evacuee from Manchester
during the air-raids on munitions factories in 1940

We quickly learned to be careful. Some of the heavier, unexploded bombs, up to 1000lbs, could create a crater twenty feet deep when set off by bomb disposal. One of these bombs could wreck an entire street, killing any inhabitants unable to find shelter. Fortunately there was never a direct hit on our road, although our adventure playground was pitted by bomb sites, great places to hide if you were part of a gang of boys.

There was a lot of playtime. If part of the school had been damaged in a raid, our gang would head for a particular bomb site where we'd established our HQ from which to plan the next escapade. There were a lot of interruptions to school lessons during the war. Most of the male teachers had been called up for military service and there were over fifty children to a class.

The classrooms were made darker by single brick walls, built directly outside to absorb imploding bomb blasts during daytime raids. When our form teacher ran out of blackboards and chalk, she would use rolls of old wallpaper and crayons. Much of what teachers had to tell us in primary school had to do with basic survival and even extended to lessons on how to make do and mend, patch and darn.

My mother often made us toffee in a baking tray, using golden syrup, sugar, cocoa and dried milk powder or condensed milk. Pea-pods as well as peas would go into a pot to make the soup go further. Young dandelion leaves, carefully washed, were used as lettuce. My grandmother's favourite drink was stinging nettles boiled into a liquid to ward off colds. She would flavour it with pulped liquorice root from Pontefract.

The kitchen in her little house…two-up-two-down with a loo in the yard, had an old coal-fired Yorkshire iron range along one wall... and that's where culinary miracles happened. My mother used to tell us that my grandmother and Aunt Annie, who lived opposite, could 'make a damned good meal out of a dish cloth.' Annie's husband, George, kept pigeons and belonged to the National Pigeon Service. Since petrol was rationed for anyone who had a car and rail travel was limited, he used his pigeons to send messages to friends a long way off. The twenty birds even had ration books: each was entitled to a weekly allowance of corn. Needless to say, it was a great treat to be in the house when any cooking or baking was to be done, because you'd be given a foretaste on a spoon of what was eventually to be dinner. Accompanying all this action in the kitchen was 'Music While You Work', a daily programme broadcast live on radio from different factories in the country, most of which were kept running by women.

There was another vital army of women during the war, The Women's Land Army. Most of the early recruits came from mill girls in Lancashire and Yorkshire, who were attracted by an outdoor life. They were a familiar sight on farms all over the country in their uniforms: thick baggy corduroy trousers, khaki smocks and khaki cloth hats.

My father was quite strict, making sure that I played my part in the household chores. We had no central heating in those days, so my main job was to keep the fires burning, which meant chopping and storing the wood. There were limited coal supplies but he showed me how to build a fire during the cold winter months, so that it would be still alight in the morning. Our bedrooms were usually freezing in winter with icicles on the inside of the windows.

My mother was a very creative cook and helped keep us warm by being able to make a meal out of almost anything. I once watched her skin a rabbit in less than a minute. We also kept chickens and spent a lot of time growing our own vegetables. I was so delighted when those vegetables which I had planted actually turned out exactly as I had hoped. There's nothing quite like tasting your own home-grown spuds. A national slogan at this time was 'Dig For Victory.' On the BBC Home Service every morning the Kitchen Front would tell the nation how to make the best of the rations they had.

Adults were required to exist weekly on 1lb of meat, 4oz of bacon, 2oz of butter, 6oz of fat, 8oz of sugar and 2oz of tea. We kept a small supply of tea, bread and tinned food in the air-raid shelter. Exempt from rationing were fish, vegetables, sausage, dried eggs and powdered milk, but these were expensive items. Sweets of any kind were rationed and so were clothes. Every person in the land was issued with a ration book and the system worked throughout the war. Neither malnutrition nor obesity became a problem. The nation was, at least, fit to fight.

Air-raid shelters of the type that people could put in the garden, if they had one, were named after their designer, John Anderson, a young civil servant in the War Department. They were dug to eight feet in depth and width. Curved steel sheets formed an arch for the roof with sandbags on top. We put earth on top of that in which we grew radishes and lettuce. These rudimentary shelters were designed to withstand a 500lb bomb going off twenty feet away... the shelters, that is, not the lettuce.

In 1940, it seemed almost certain that Hitler would waste no time in crossing the channel, having swept through France and Belgium and so it was decided to make life as difficult as possible for the invaders when they tried to blast their way through England. All signposts were removed, including milestones, from one end of the country to the other. Fake military positions set up using dummy soldiers and telegraph poles were made to look like anti-aircraft guns. I suspect this might have been a ruse dreamed up by the Capt. Mannering of the Home Guard. Luckily for us Hitler changed his mind about the timing of his invasion plan for England and decided to invade Russia instead. He probably thought Britain would be a pushover and we could wait a while longer. He was so confident about conquering England he had even sent his Minister for Propaganda, Josef Goebbels to West Sussex in 1939 … before war had been declared … to explore a few stately homes suitable for the Fuehrer. A photograph of a smiling Goebbels can still be seen above the bar in the Spread Eagle Hotel at Midhurst, near Chichester. Anyway, that decision to postpone the invasion of our shores certainly gave our country vital breathing space.

National publicity left no stone unturned to help the war effort. Someone calculated that the aluminium from milk bottle tops, if saved and collected by the milkman every week, could produce fifty Lancaster bombers. Old wellington boots could be turned into jumping boots for paratroops. A six-inch length of old wool collected from all the knitters in the country could make six hundred sets of battle dress for the army, while 250,000 razor blades thrown away each day could produce ninety tons of metal. Rag and bone lorries driven by the WVS (Women's Voluntary Service) were used to collect it all.

Lord Haw-Haw was an American-born fascist politician and Nazi broadcaster to the United Kingdom during World War II. His real name was William Joyce. He took German citizenship in 1940 and became Josef Goebbels' number one propagandist broadcasting from Hamburg, always with the opening line… "This is Germany calling…This is Germany calling…" I often heard him pinpoint individual streets in Manchester that were due for destruction, he warned, in the next bombing raid.

Joyce was captured by allied forces in Northern Germany after his last broadcast in 1945 and brought back to England. He was hanged on 3rd January 1946, the last person to be executed for treason in the United Kingdom.

CHAPTER 3

THE DIE IS CAST

By the time the war ended I was twelve and had already decided that somehow I would become a reporter. I still longed to impress Barbara Walton, the girl in our street, but she was now crazy about some movie star called Alan Ladd whom she'd seen portraying an all-action journalist. That clinched it for me. I was not going to be outdone by a pint-sized squirt like Alan Ladd. As it happened, my Aunt Annie in Wakefield had a lodger, Geoff Hemingway, who was a real reporter on a local evening paper. Whenever I visited my aunt, I listened to him talking about his stories to his news editor and he explained to me what I would have to do if I was really serious about journalism as a career. On his advice I began learning Pitman's shorthand with such determination that, by the time I was sixteen, I had become quite proficient.

My father, away with the army, knew nothing of this ambition of mine. I think he had hoped that I might follow in his footsteps and join the police force. He had been promoted to the rank of Major and at the end of the war became involved in the slow process of 'denazifying' the Ruhr. He started the first training school for a new German police force in Wuppertal, which meant he had to personally vet every single recruit. There were so many ex-Nazis trying to hide their past: for them a new police force was obviously worth a try, but for my father it involved a huge workload of interrogations and investigations. He had a team of interpreters led by a multilingual Dutch woman, Anne-Marie Zimmerman, who became the only person he trusted, along with his army dog, Carlo who never left his side.

The de-nazification programme kept my father in Germany until well after the war was over, so by the time he returned to police duty in England I was making my first moves towards becoming a cub reporter. I had taken the School Certificate equivalent to GCSE O-level and had unilaterally decided that my sixteenth year was going to be my last in formal education. My father was unaware of this, or that I had already written to several weekly papers up and down the country. I had been rejected by all of them as being 'too young to be away from home' and 'did my parents know what I was doing?'

I hid these letters away carefully, until one day I spotted an advertisement in the UK Press Gazette offering an opening for a trainee journalist on the Ashton-under-Lyne Reporter, based near Manchester. Although it was three buses and a tram ride away from where I lived, in Fallowfield South Manchester, a good hour and a half journey, it was exactly what I wanted. I sent off another letter and was so very excited when I received a reply, asking me to go for an interview. I could not keep the good news from my mother, but still did not tell my father. He thought I would be continuing my formal education. But the die was cast.

The newspaper's old red-brick building dominated the Market Square in the centre of Ashton-under-Lyne. The 'Reporter' had a large circulation, stretching from the Peak District to the outskirts of Oldham and into Manchester city centre. From the moment I stepped into the building I was in love with the smell of print. As I was ushered into the office of the news editor, Jack Middlehurst, I had a strong feeling that this was going to be the right place for me. I felt well prepared for the interview, armed with my own shorthand notebook tucked inside my jacket. Jack was an avuncular figure but straight talking: very proud of his newspaper. He told me about all the successful reporters who had cut their teeth there, including Harold Evans who went on to become the legendary editor of The Sunday Times.

'I notice in your letter you say you have shorthand,' he said to me, cutting straight to the chase. He offered me a book of lined paper and a pencil. 'Take this down'. With which he picked up a copy of that day's Manchester Guardian. I already had my own notebook ready on my lap.

'Now read it back,' he said when he had finished reading out the chosen article. Fortunately it was not a long piece and I was able to quote it verbatim. His face told me he was impressed, so far. He asked me about my school and why I had left so early and whether my parents were happy about what I was doing.

He then explained that the job really amounted to a three-year apprenticeship, approved by the National Union of Journalists and went on to ask me if I was ready for that kind of commitment. Could I cope with the long journey each day from home requiring me to be at the office by 8am? It was my first formal job interview and I had no idea, by the time Jack had finished grilling me, how well it had really gone. He thanked me for coming and said I would hear from him within two days. He shook my hand but gave no indication as to whether he was pleased or not. As I left, one of the reporters in the newsroom said, 'Don't look so worried. He doesn't usually talk to interviewees for that long, son. Best of luck'.

Although optimistic, I was on tenterhooks for the next few days, waiting for the letter that might determine my destiny. There was also the problem of how I was going to tell my father that I had left school. He was away on a two-week course at Hendon Police College when my interview came up. Anyway the letter from Ashton, as promised, came through the door within two days. 'Dear David, I am pleased to be able to offer you a position on our Journalist Training Scheme...at a salary of 28 shillings a week...' What a thrill it was receiving that letter and although my mother shared in my excitement, I could tell that she too was concerned about my father's reaction. I tried not to worry. I was successfully getting a foot on the first rung of the ladder.

The first few weeks were spent in the Reading Room where Bob Hall, a kindly retired English teacher, took me through the painstaking business of proof-reading and marking columns of type for errors, before sending them back to the compositors; through him I learned about each stage of the newspaper's production. All the reporters had very good shorthand which they needed for covering the likes of council meetings and magistrates' court hearings. Every lunch hour I honed my Pitmans skills with Eddie Ingram, a little man with a big heart, who taught me a lot about constructing a story. Though he was unusually short in height he was very fast on his feet. He played football well and wrote passionately about cricket, his favourite sport. He and I became lifelong friends. I had just finished my second week on the paper when my father returned from Hendon. I was sitting at the kitchen table studying various books I'd been given on journalism. Fortunately my mother had been able to forewarn my father when he got home. He just sat down opposite me and looking very stern said: 'What the hell's going on then...?' I plucked up my courage.

'I've started work on a newspaper. They've offered me a place on a training scheme.' I had fully expected that he would tell me I could forget about it; instead he asked which newspaper it was.

'The Ashton-under-Lyne Reporter,' I told him.

'Ashton bloody under Lyne,' he shouted, as though it was somewhere in outer space. 'That's not even Manchester.'

To which I replied, 'Only two buses and a tram ride away'.

'I don't give a bugger! Why didn't you discuss this with me before just going ahead off your own bat. You're only sixteen.'

I told him it was because I knew he would try to stop me. The best way to start, I told him, was on a good weekly newspaper and if he wanted some reassurance he could ask his contacts on the national dailies how they got their jobs. He could also check with Jack Middlehurst, who would be only too happy to explain just what the training scheme entailed. It took a while, but eventually my father abandoned all efforts to steer me into a 'worthwhile' profession. He knew that National Service was only a year or so away and thought that maybe it would knock some sense into me.

Births, marriages and deaths are bread and butter events to a weekly paper. Apart from the advertising they attract a lot of people, especially in working class districts such as Openshaw and Gorton, which I was assigned to cover.

With everyone struggling to get back on their feet after the ravages of war, the only way to get to know the local people was to get down there and mix with them, so the local police, the fire brigade and church ministers were among my daily calls: not phone calls, but personal visits so that they could put a face to my name, feel confident about talking to me and hopefully call me if something interesting happened, or better still, was about to happen.

I got used to knocking on people's doors when there had been a death in the family and not be too frightened to ask questions about the life that had passed. Despite the grief that relatives felt, they invariably gave their time willingly to the local reporter so that their loved one's time on earth, however ordinary, could be given a good write-up.

I learnt how to get the best out of an otherwise humdrum story, but there were also a few wonderful exceptions: unsung heroes who had gone through hell on the Somme and never breathed a word about it, their reward being a medal and others who maybe received a gold watch for thirty loyal years service in a factory.

The paper printed on a Thursday, when we were usually given the afternoon off to make up for all the weekends and evenings we had worked. The news editor, Jack Middlehurst, collared me one Thursday and handed me a package. 'Take this to Mr. Clegg, the undertaker, on your way home, if you would, he's a big advertiser with us.' Clegg's funeral parlour had a large frontage on Ashton Old Road, Openshaw: he was one of the undertakers I had yet to meet. He had a broad Lancashire accent but tried to sound posh, putting 'aitches where there were none. He was as bald as a coot, quite short and nervy, blinking a lot. I handed him the package and he asked if I had a driving licence. I nodded: 'Yes. Passed the test quite recently.'

'I'll give you a quid if you'd drive one of t'cars in a job this afternoon. I'm a man short.' I jumped at the chance. A quid was a lot to me then. He looked painfully at the check jacket I was wearing.

'You can't go looking like that lad. Come in't back and we'll fix you up.' From a rack of long black funeral coats which were all the fashion, he held one up. 'Try this,' he said. 'It'll be a bit short in't sleeves but it'll do. Folk won't be looking at you anyway.' Fair enough, I was only going to be driving a car. The car in question was a huge Austen 20, with a glass screen separating the driver from the passengers and the choke, I noticed, was a makeshift toggle attached to a piece of wire hanging from under the dashboard. Mr Clegg gave it a tug and turned the engine over. It growled like a lion.

'There you go. Good as gold.' I didn't find his confidence reassuring and when it came time to pick up the coffin and mourners, my car was the last one in the line. Some of the mourners scrambled into the rear, unaware of the difficulty I was having restarting the car. The choke, full out, had probably flooded the carburettor and so it was a few minutes before I got the engine ticking over again. None of the mourners had yet noticed that we were still stationary or that the cortege was way ahead, had already reached the main road, turned left and was now out of sight.

Luckily, the engine on my huge tank of a car decided to behave and we were off at last. Ashton Old Road was busy, so we had to overtake quite a few cars to make up ground. The passengers didn't seem too perturbed as we weaved in and out of the traffic. They were just rolling rather heavily from side to side but the cortege, still well ahead of me now crossed some traffic lights.

We were a long way behind and stuck at the red lights. There was only one thing for it, to take a shortcut. I turned the tank quickly into a narrow side street, a factory on one side and terraced houses on the other. Women chatting on their doorsteps looked alarmed as the great black car roared by. Halfway down the cobbled street I realised it was a dead end. I couldn't possibly manage a three-point turn in this beast of a vehicle, there just wasn't enough room. Besides, I was late. We were almost at the end of the street and there was a sudden bump: before I knew it, we had mounted the kerb and were bouncing over what seemed like a strange moonscape full of rubbish, buckets and abandoned mattresses everywhere. It was a really rocky ride. Now I had my passengers' full attention. One elderly lady banged on the window behind me.

'Young man,' she shouted, 'I do think you ought to stick wit' main procession.' Too late for that luv', I said to myself as we ploughed on to the other side of the wasteland, crashing down onto tarmac road again. Now we were in with a chance. An old man in the back shouted:

'It's not a bloody steeplechase lad!' We raced on to the cemetery, through the big iron gates and up the hill to the crematorium. Everyone got out and started looking around for familiar faces. There wasn't a living soul to be seen. I began to wonder whether I had brought them to the wrong cemetery. It seemed like an eternity before I eventually caught sight of the hearse coming up the hill.

Mr Clegg, in the passenger seat of the hearse, did not look happy. He could see me leaning casually on the side of my car, looking pleased with myself. As he got closer I could see he was really agitated about something. I thought he would be relieved that I was there in one piece. But as soon as he'd reached us, he rushed over to my passengers apologising, then turned his anger on me.

'H'i 'ave been in't business forty years son and this takes the bloody cake. You're not supposed to get 'ere first. Its not a bloody race to t' grave. Go and 'elp Harry.'

He gestured toward the tallest of three men standing by the hearse. Harry was a pin-smart, sergeant majorly figure, who seemed keen to take me through the drill of removing the coffin.

'As you can see it sits on runners. When my mate at the front gives it a bit of shove, you bend slightly and put your right shoulder under it.' Harry ran through the actions again and told me to get ready. I was braced, in the slips as it were, when the coffin came hurtling towards me. Harry's mate at front must have given it more than a bit of a shove. It came out like a missile and hit me square in the chest, sending me flat. Harry quickly helped me up and dusted me off.

The funeral director on the other hand was bordering on apoplectic, judging by his ruddy face, but he obviously didn't want to cause a scene in front of all the mourners, so he just stayed silent. Somehow he sent puffs of spray in my direction, while gesturing to Harry to get a grip on the situation.

Sergeant-major Harry put me at the rear end of the coffin, but as luck would have it the other three men were much taller than me: the only way I could keep the coffin level was to practically stand on tiptoe. There was no-one else to call upon so they decided to make the best of it. The walk to the graveside was agonising and I had a terrible thought that at any moment the coffin would topple over, the lid would fall off and out would roll the dear departed. I could feel the mourners willing me to make a mess of it, but after what seemed like an eternity, the coffin was laid to rest without further complications.

All I now had to do was deliver the mourners back to the funeral parlour unscathed; no-one spoke a word on the journey. Not even a flicker of appreciation. The miserable buggers were going to leave it to Clegg to give me a bollocking. Once safely back at base they just left, without even a thank you.

I parked the big car and was about to walk to the funeral parlour to collect my well-earned money when a weary feeling came over me. I had done enough for one day. To hell with the quid. I hurried away and caught the bus home. It was a long night though, worrying about repercussions the next day, as there surely would be. At worst, it might mean the end of my career in journalism. I didn't mention to my parents what had actually happened. Next day, I was full of trepidation when I went into the newspaper office. As soon as I reached the newsroom, one of the reporters said ominously: 'Jack wants to see you in his office right away.' Fair enough. Time to face the music. Jack Middlehurst's face was set, hard, uncompromising.

'I have spent an hour on the phone listening to a very irate Mr

Clegg and I have never known him so angry. He has told me everything about your antics yesterday in minute detail. What a terrifying experience it was for the mourners. He has left nothing out… and I have to tell you…' This is it, I thought, I am going to be fired.

'I have to tell you, David,' he said slowly, emphasising every word, 'I have never heard anything in my life quite SO BLOODY FUNNY!' With that he burst out laughing. What a relief. When he'd composed himself he explained that because Mr Clegg's advertising was so important I would need to grovel a little. I would need to gather my courage, confront him and offer him an apology. 'No maybes, just do it. A little bullshit makes the world go around,' Jack said with a wink. It wasn't easy being the butt of everyone's jokes for the rest of the day, but the important thing was that I still had a job.

It wasn't just a job, it had become more a way of life, to the extent that I didn't have a normal teenage existence. For most of the time I was working: even at weekends there were always events to cover with a photographer. It took a lot of material to fill up an entire edition of the paper and when I wasn't out on the road, I was writing up the stories to send to the printers as early as possible.

The friends I had from school had lost touch with me because I was never available and in any case I didn't earn enough money to go out drinking with them. That didn't really worry me. I was steeped in newspapers. Sex had so far eluded me although my father did make one brief attempt to bring me into the loop. 'Always wear a condom,' he advised gravely. That was all the information I got. For a while, whenever I was near a Boots chemist, I would go in with the intention of asking for help, but the women assistants always looked so stern that my courage failed me at the last minute, with the result that I finished up buying yet another comb. I had enough combs to set up a stall. I finally realised that in those days Boots didn't even sell condoms. You had to buy them at a barber's shop. There were signs for all to see…'Durex'.

So I went for a trim I didn't really need. Once finished, the barber said: 'would you like something for the weekend, sir?' It took a few seconds for the penny to drop. I mumbled a few words, trying to make it sound as though 'something for the weekend' and I were well acquainted. I left the shop clutching the vital battle rations. All I needed to do now was to find a girl.

I had hoped it might be Zoe, a lovely girl I'd met from Wakefield. I liked her very much but got the impression that there'd be no sex before marriage; either that or she was a little shy. Or both. She once came to my grandmother's house in Wakefield when I was on a weekend visit. It was early and I hadn't yet got out of bed. She volunteered to cook bacon and eggs for my breakfast and was offered the run of the kitchen. Zoe confidently got on with the cooking and when she was done, showed my grandmother the frying pan. All was perfect – except for one burnt black speck right in the centre of the yoke:

'How's that?' asked Zoe.

'Oh Dear!' my grandmother said. 'He can't stand a mucky egg.'

Unfortunately Zoe and I never got close to sex. It was nothing to do with the mucky egg; she lived in Wakefield and I was in Manchester. We continued our trans-Pennine friendship by letter, half in longhand and half in shorthand because we were both trying to improve our Pitmans. Useful, but not very romantic, though there was always the hope that, one day, something magical might happen.

The most important thing to me at the time was the valuable experience I was gaining at work. Weekly journalism may seem mundane but it teaches how to get facts straight and sharpens the nose for a story. Occasionally, I came into contact with some reporters on the national dailies that were printed in Manchester, but their lives seemed so far removed from mine. They smoked heavily, drank a lot and professed to know more about the nightlife of the city than any others I'd ever known. That wasn't saying much for a teenager like me, still wet behind the ears, dutifully plodding around my 'patch' for the weekly paper.

Amazingly, a few of them could sit in a pub and write a story almost completely inebriated. When they came to file their pieces on the pub phone I could barely recognise the story as I knew it. Their stories were so full of drama. Where the hell had I been to have missed so much? Or had I? You know the old saying: never let the facts get in the way of a good story.

In those early days, I was fortunate to have become friends with two journalists who became my mentors, Harold

Pendlebury and Vincent Mulchrone on the Daily Mail, when it was a highly respected broadsheet. My father, still a police inspector, had brought Vincent home with him one night when he was stuck for somewhere to live and he stayed for a year or so. By then we had moved up-market to a large house in Kedleston Avenue, Victoria Park with my sisters: Hilary who was four years younger than me and had already set her sights on becoming an actress and little Margaret who was just a toddler.

During that time I was hardened into the ruthless business of getting a story, while also developing a personal style of writing. Working on a national newspaper was extremely competitive: in the 1950s you would not even be considered unless you came with some tried and tested experience in provincial journalism on a reputable newspaper along with the cuttings to prove it.

Harold Pendlebury was tirelessly determined about uncovering all the facts of a story, not just a few nuggets: he just wouldn't stop until he'd got what he was after. Not surprisingly reporters on opposition papers were terrified when they discovered they were on the same story as Harold. Vincent Mulchrone was in a league of his own. His Yorkshire grit and Irish charm put him well ahead of the pack. I was privileged to watch the effort he put into writing his articles, which made them such a pleasure to read, some of them composed in the evening at our kitchen table. One of his fans was the Queen. Apparently, when he covered Royal tours later on in his career, she would want to know what Mulchrone had to say each day. His pieces were always out of the ordinary, so rich in wit and humour.

These two journalists, Pendlebury and Mulchrone, helped to set the course I was to take later, once I had finished my National Service. They became lifetime friends, always on the end of a phone when I needed their advice. Vincent once told me: 'On a big story, don't forget to watch out for the little people. Find out what are they're doing.' I think that was why his writing on Royal tours was so popular with the Queen. She could read what some of her loyal subjects were really doing. Thanks to Vincent Mulchrone my father began to change his mind about journalists. For a start, he could see that to do it well was bloody hard work and discovered that they weren't all unscrupulous con-artists. He was prepared to accept that there just might be a few exceptions.

CHAPTER 4

NATIONAL SERVICE

Britain was still in the throes of post-war recovery when I was called up, barely eighteen, never having put a foot on foreign soil. We had soldiers involved in jungle warfare fighting the Mau Mau uprising where the Kikuyu tribe, led by Jomo Kenyatta, were ferociously demanding independence from British rule. More jungle warfare lingering on in Malaysia against colonial forces. In Korea, as part of a UN force, we were battling Chinese communist troops against overwhelming odds.

The safest bet for a young National Serviceman was to be ordered to serve in Germany as part of BAOR (British Army on the Rhine). I had been warned that I would not get any say in where I might be posted, but ever hopeful I had started learning German, sometime before the fateful letter came, summoning me to Aldershot in Hampshire.

The last words from my father were: 'Try to get a job as a driver. That way, wherever you finish up, you'll be able to keep dry.' Sounded like good advice I thought, I'll go for that; but you didn't just turn up at a British army training barracks and tell them what you had in mind to do. I tried, but a bull of a sergeant major, who I thought was there to welcome me after I had travelled all the way from Manchester, looked at me as though I was something foul he'd picked up on his shoe.

'Over there,' he growled, pointing to a long line of maybe a hundred or so young men who had come from all over the country, from the city, from the plough, a rag-bag mixture of teenage specimens with accents I could barely decipher, all looking lost and confused as though they'd been dropped onto another planet. We were all lined up at the quartermaster's store and given denim overalls, known as 'fatigues' before being led to a series of barrack blocks where we were told to change and parcel up our civilian clothes for posting home: we were not going to need them for some time.

Some of this motley collection, I discovered, had already been behind bars for violent crimes and regarded National Service as a kind of gap year and others obviously couldn't even write their own names and addresses properly. A few were completely illiterate and had got by so far by delegation and intimidation. I started to wonder what was going to happen if they all wanted to be drivers: perhaps I'd be better off in the infantry! Within a few days we had all been kitted out with battledress, boots and webbing and shorn to within a millimetre of our scalps. No-one wanted to be seen outside the camp, even if that had been possible. There were already signs that quite a few of these neanderthals were not going to accept a life of strict discipline without trouble. But the time-serving regulars, corporals and sergeants assigned to each barracks, had seen it all before and were not going to take any shit from anyone. It appeared that we were not humans to them, just a name and number. I was now 22864271 Tindall D. Six weeks of square-bashing, exercises and cold showers followed, before we would learn what else the army might have in store for us.

There were a few written tests, not at all difficult, but even so I noticed a lot of vacant stares and blank pages. Some of us were given interviews with an officer in which the sort of work we had been doing in civvy street was discussed. A few days after my interview I was informed that I was being moved to Maresfield Park Camp, near Uckfield in Sussex.

'Never heard of it, what happens there?' I asked, but no-one could or would tell me.

'You'll find out when you get there,' an officer said. 'Here's your travel warrant.'

Within a couple of hours I was among the mellow rolling downs of Sussex. Maresfield Park Camp was very quiet, tucked away from public view, a far cry from the busy garrison town of Aldershot. I reported to the Commanding Officer, Major Hawkins, who sat in a book-lined office and wore civilian clothes. He politely offered me a seat and explained that I had arrived at the headquarters of the Intelligence Corps.

'I think someone might have made a mistake sir,' I said.

'Well, we will be the judge of that,' he retorted.

During the next few weeks there was weapons training, some target practice but only a minimal amount of square-bashing: just enough to make sure we could all walk in a straight line. The rest of the time it was rather like being back at school, except that I really enjoyed these lessons which were an introduction to the fascinating world of espionage and the role of the Intelligence Corps. My fellow students were an interesting mixture of academics, some who had deferred their entrance to university. One had worked in film production and some had even run their own companies.

If we made the grade, we were to be sent abroad, so by now the idea of being a driver had vanished. There was a much more exciting life on the horizon, pure John Le Carre: that is if the powers that be were ever going to allow a bunch of National Servicemen anywhere near anything hush-hush.

Anyway, I passed with an A grade, signed the Official Secrets Act and was told I would be posted to Germany where I would be based in Dusseldorf, assigned to100 FSS (100 Field Security Section, Intelligence Corps). Some in my class had gone into the cyphers and signals branch, a few were to spend their National Service learning Russian and yet others went to Trieste on the Adriatic, then a listening post during the Cold War with the Soviet Union. At the end of WWII, only seven years earlier, the USSR had divided Europe with what Churchill dubbed the 'Iron Curtain', a non-physical boundary line that stretched from Stettin in the Baltic to Trieste on the Adriatic.

Top right, second row down, one in from the right, is me, aged 18 doing my National Service with 100 Field Security Section, Intelligence Corps, in Dusseldorf, Germany

I had never been abroad before. Along the quayside at Harwich were a few hundred of us from different units throughout Britain waiting to board a troopship to the Hook of Holland from where we would continue into Germany. All of us were in uniform, except for one tall, bespectacled young man in a white pullover, who loped casually along the dockside carrying nothing but a tennis racket, as though this boat trip had rudely interrupted his day. An angry sergeant stopped him in his tracks and bellowed:

'What do you think this is soldier, your daddy's fucking yacht. Why are you not in uniform?' There came an unconcerned reply:

'Oh! I've had all that stuff posted on ahead of me sergeant … bit of a fag having to cart it all around.' This guy was straight out of P.G. Wodehouse, I thought, I like him. Maybe he's sent Jeeves on ahead as well. The young man's name was Bill Boyd and luckily we were being posted to the same unit in the Intelligence Corps. It was a rough sea in a jam-packed ship, but Boyd took it all in his stride, saying 'So this is what it's like in steerage.'

The boat seemed to be full of young soldiers ready to start World War III if anyone so much as looked at them the wrong way, like Viking recruits prepared to rip your head off just for the fun of it. I was glad when we reached Holland and were on the train to the Rhine.

No 34, Roland Strasse was a redbrick three-storey block of flats with a large basement garage, pretty much like any other building in the quiet middle-class district of Dusseldorf off Kaiserswertherstrtasse, which ran along the Rhine into town. There seemed to be a lot of comings and goings in the evenings, mostly at weekends, young men driving smart grey-coloured Volkswagens, when the sound of people enjoying themselves could be heard coming from the rear of the building, which had its own secluded walled garden.

Overlooking the garden was a large room with a plate-glass window stretching from side to side. This was 'The Bar': its secrets known only to a select few in the British Army on the Rhine. Any outsiders who were favoured with an invitation to enjoy the hospitality were sworn to secrecy, which did not work very well. Rooms containing classified documents were always locked and protected. It was just The Bar that was the attraction and as a result it was a big money-spinner, funding an extraordinary life-style for its residents. 100 Section somehow managed to acquire 34 Roland Strasse: it had been the brainchild of our entrepreneurial Staff-Sergeant Jan Brochwicz

Lewinsky, who approached a local German brewery and persuaded them to set up a bar on the premises and to keep it fully stocked at all times. Whatever credit was due to the brewery for their initial outlay would be paid back from the profits. Before long the profits were so large that 34 Roland Strasse could afford to hire a housekeeper, a cook, odd-job-men and a gardener. It was a unique little corner of the British Army.

Brochwicz was also doing such a roaring trade in black market booze in Dusseldorf that he could have sent us all on holiday to Biarritz. The weekend parties in The Bar could be rowdy and the big glass window overlooking the garden was so frequently smashed that we eventually employed a local man to be on more or less permanent standby. One evening when our man came to repair the broken window while a party was still going on, a warrant officer visiting us from another part of Germany was so impressed he asked how a guy appeared like that just appeared out of nowhere. Brochwicz said: 'Oh! He's our duty glazier!' It was important that whatever damage had been caused the night before, come the morning, all had to be ship-shape and ready for inspection, should that ever happen.

One of 100 Section's more sober roles was counter-espionage: weeding out illegals, crossing the frontier from Soviet-controlled East Germany, whose mission was to gain work in British army workshops dealing with the latest weapons and to report back to their Communist masters. That job entailed sifting through every German's application for work in the British army and then checking for flaws in their story; a long, tedious process which rarely turned up trumps.

The records of all civilians who had been on the payroll of the British army since the end of the war were stored in the Stahlhof, a huge early 20th century administrative building in Dusseldorf which, as the name implies, looks like a turreted red-stone fortress. During the war it had been the Rhineland Administrative HQ of the Waffen SS, headed by Heinrich Himmler. Now, here I was, occasionally on night duty in this vast spooky building, which my father told me he had helped to clear of remaining Nazis as they tried to destroy their files towards the end of the war. One of his trophies from that raid was a gold clock which he had taken from the office of a German officer who had shot himself rather than be captured. It stood on a mantelpiece in our house back in England for many years.

When climbing up the wide spiral staircase in the Stahlhof, the eyes of stern-looking civic leaders over the decades followed each step from enormous oil paintings. I imagined that I could still hear the echo of jackboots pounding the floors in Hitler's time, which wasn't that long ago. After the war the British army, apart from storing records there, used the building as a courthouse. In the 1950s, a staff-sergeant named Emmet-Dunne was tried in this court for murdering the husband of a woman with whom he was having an affair. Though the death penalty still existed in Britain, the case ended with a sentence to life imprisonment.

One night, while on duty in Stahlhof, I delved into our regional intelligence files for anything on Anne-Marie Zimmerman, my father's Dutch-born interpreter during the war. Lo and behold, there she was, with a current address in Dusseldorf. I made contact with her and she invited me to lunch. She was a beautiful woman: tall, with long auburn hair and made no secret of her affection for my father. I left our very congenial lunch with the feeling that Anne-Marie and he had enjoyed more than just a close working relationship. He had often spoken to me about her and how important she had been while portraying her, at least to my mother, as a rather ample, cottage-loaf German hausfrau. I can't blame him for that, knowing my mother's quick temper. Surprisingly, Anne-Marie Zimmerman was listed in our current files as being a member of the German Communist Party, though not classified as any risk so far as the British army was concerned.

Part of our field work was to carry out periodic spot checks on security at British army units. I usually got my assignments from Jan Brochwicz, a real soldier I reckoned, who had earned his medals in combat during the war. He'd been in the Polish cavalry when Germany invaded his country and then managed to escape to England to join the British army. As a paratrooper, part of his face had been shot away while charging a German trench. He was sent to England as a patient of Archibald McIndoe, the plastic surgeon, who was doing amazing work on badly burned RAF pilots at Queen Victoria Hospital, East Grinstead. He did such a wonderful job on Jan that I could only see the scars of his plastic surgery when he turned sideways.

When McIndoe had finished with him, Jan returned to active

soldiering as a tank commander in a cavalry unit serving in Palestine. But one day, so the story went, he cornered some Jewish freedom fighters in a house and instead of taking them prisoner ordered his tank to open fire. The house disintegrated, apparently killing everyone in it. Jan was demoted and drummed out of his regiment. But some of those, who had served with him in Palestine and on the battlefield in Germany, considered that the army hierarchy should not lose such an experienced soldier and that with his language skills, Russian, French, German and Polish, he would be valuable and perhaps less harmful in peacetime field security work. So, here he was, a Staff sergeant in the Intelligence Corps, with a little booze business on the side. But Jan liked thoroughness and encouraged us National Service wallahs to be bold in our approach to field security work.

On one job, Ricky Stoakes and myself were to do a 'night check' on the offices of a British armaments unit which employed Jugoslav guards. All went well until we were approaching the building across a concrete pathway which had rubber strips dividing it. Suddenly all the lights around us went on and we were totally exposed. At one end, two guards appeared with German shepherd dogs straining at the leash. No-one had mentioned anything about dogs. Terrified, we ran as fast as we could to a brick wall about ten-feet high. Normally, we would have had difficulty getting over, but on this occasion we seemed to fly up and over the top, onto a railway siding with empty carriages. We opened one and hid inside. Meanwhile the dogs and their guards had found a way round the side and were on us in minutes.

'Raus ... out,' one of the guards shouted. The dogs, teeth bared, looked as though they were ready to rip us to pieces. Through the window we made it clear that we were not moving until they put these animals on their chains. Thankfully, the guards eventually did just that and we cautiously stepped down; even so I was still petrified that we'd finish up in shreds. Fortunately, the guards could see we were unarmed and not much of a threat. They arrested us and took us to their checkpoint at the front gate. We explained who we were, what the hell we were supposed to be doing and gave them a number to call our boss, Jan Brochwicz. When he came to pick us up he thought it was all a bit of a laugh. 'They nearly had you for breakfast, boys.' The moral of this story, I guess, is to do your homework well before you act. Fools rush in where angels fear to tread.

From time to time, I would be engaged in field security work well away from our Dusseldorf base. For a while, I was attached to the Black Watch at Iserlohn, a medieval town in North Rhine-Westphalia, south-east of Dortmund. The regiment had recently returned from duty in Kenya during the Mau Mau uprising, along with some troops from the Lancashire Fusiliers and they brought the signs of bloody jungle warfare with them. The Fusiliers normally had bright yellow hackles on their berets but when they went on parade in Iserlohn, these plumes were stained deep red.

The Black Watch had been confined to barracks because there had been a few fights and there was a nervousness among the civilian population over scare stories about the skirl of the pipes and the kilted soldiers from hell. But the regiment did its best to put the local people more at ease, laying on a full-dress pipe and drum parade through town. Hundreds of Germans turning out to see the Black Watch in all its glory, for what was a great example in public relations.

Throughout my service in Germany I never had any luck with the frauleins, not that they were queueing up to meet us… just the opposite. I never met any German girl who showed the slightest interest in English lads. Mind you, at the time, although I was twenty I only looked about fifteen. My one and only chance to finally experience the life force came towards the end of my time, when I met an English girl who lived in Dusseldorf with her family… her dad, I believe, was in the prison service. One weekend when they were away she invited me back to her home. Passions were running high. This was it. I had the army-issue condoms in my pocket. We kissed our way into the bedroom and onto a wonderful double bed. Off came the clothes, we pressed together, barely a thin layer of talc between us, ready to go, when I remembered my father's words: 'always use a French letter…' That's all he had advised, no other pearls of wisdom. It was enough for me to pause at the thought of an unwanted pregnancy and I said: 'wait just a moment.' Agonising minutes passed while I fiddled about like a fool, making a botch of it until the poor girl, clearly irritated by now, said 'Just get on with it.'

I was desperate, trying to steady myself on one hand while fumbling about with the other but lost my balance. I fell forward, cracking my head on the wall. 'What the hell's going on?' the girl asked, to which my pathetic reply was: 'What do you think I am: a bloody contortionist.' It's surprising how quickly passion can disappear, along with wishful hopes for the future. Maybe I was destined to be the only bloke ever to finish his National Service still a virgin.

CHAPTER 5

BACK TO CIVVY STREET

While I had been away my father considered retiring from the police force after twenty-five years and to please my mother was now taking a course in hotel management. She wanted him to do something in which she could become involved. At the end of the war he'd been offered promotion and a permanent staff job in the army, but my mother had not wanted to move to Germany. It was a difficult decision for him, not just because of the lost prospects but because he didn't want to abandon his army dog, Carlo. When he had to leave Carlo with his successor, the pining animal ran off into the forest and went feral. For months after he had returned to Britain my father fantasised that somehow the dog would find its way onto a troopship and miraculously turn up at the front door.

My father now took the decision to leave the police force, despite being offered promotion to be Chief Constable of York: a really big opportunity. It was more important to him that my mother be happy. When I first heard I thought he was mad, but he really loved his wife and family. He told my youngest sister Margaret, in later life, that when he came back from the army he'd discovered that he was not her father, but he always cared for her as though she was his own and I never knew any different. Margaret thinks her real father was an American soldier.

Anyway, after National Service I found myself in Stoke-on-Trent, where my father successfully turned his hand to being a publican, being next offered The Peel Arms Hotel at Tamworth, one of the nicest coaching inns in Staffordshire, giving my mother her chance to shine as the glamorous hostess. Margaret, still at school, was living with them.

One weekend, when I was visiting, a fire broke out in the middle of the night in an upstairs sitting room. It had apparently been simmering for hours before the roof collapsed, taking the budgerigar with it and belching smoke and flames out into the corridor. I dashed upstairs to the room next door where Margaret was sleeping. I grabbed her and crawled back along the corridor just below the smoke level, meeting a fireman in a mask coming the other way. A close call. It took months to restore the place.

The Potteries is rightly proud of its global reputation for producing fine china, but it's a long way off Mecca when it comes to journalism. There were no vacancies on the Sentinel, the sole evening paper. I hadn't yet gained the experience required to get a job on a daily paper. Catch 22: how do you get the experience in the first place? For a while I took work in a tile factory as a trainee salesman, which involved a lot of careful arithmetic, my worst subject even with great concentration. Somehow they persevered with me, despite my repeated miscalculations. An old hand remarked that 'by the time we've finished with yer, yer'll be able to sell forty cans of beans to a bloke who wants a second-hand motor-bike.' But they seemed sure of my potential as a 'rep', so I was to be schooled from the factory floor onwards and sent to pottery evening classes at the local technical college. In the 1950s, there were hundreds of young ladies on the factory floor and the appearance of any newcomer in trousers set them shrieking. A twenty-year-old single male was fair game. They'd have your trousers off in no time. Time was something I didn't want to waste. I still wanted to get back on track with my career in journalism and eventually convinced my very patient boss at the factory that tiles weren't really for me. I briefly took a reporting job on a small family weekly in Stoke, The City Times.

Throughout my service in Germany I had continued my postal relationship with Zoe from Wakefield and now that I was back home she wanted to visit me in Stoke, which coincided with a new love in my life … Mary Geraldine. 'Gerry' was once Carnival Queen of Great Britain, with gorgeous long legs. She knew all about condoms and at last I entered the real world. Well that's a new way of putting it: I was madly in love. I broke up with Zoe when she came to see me and sadly I heard that she had cried all the way home. Her mother wrote me a stinging letter… 'handsome is, as handsome does' was her acid comment.

Gerry fulfilled all my dreams. I was thrilled that we would be together as I moved on with my career but I was still very young and relatively inexperienced as a journalist: but a chance did come. I answered an advertisement in the UK Press Gazette for an experienced reporter, minimum age 25, on the Gloucester-shire Echo, an evening paper in Cheltenham. This time, I was going to take a leaf out Harold Pendlebury's book: be bold. I bought a pair of horn-rimmed spectacles with plain glass in them and applied for the job, hopefully looking five years older than my real age. The next day I caught a train to Cheltenham. I told the receptionist at The Echo that I just happened to be doing some work in their area and thought I would call in to see if the editor was free for a chat. Fortunately he was, so I walked into his office wearing my new specs.

Mr Hollinshead was an old-fashioned character, very much the English gentleman whose great passion was cricket. We got on well. There were piles of letters on his desk which I assumed were applications for the job. I was on form that day. Half-an-hour later Mr Hollinshead told me he would take a chance and offered me the job on six months trial. He put me in charge of a new district office in Evesham where I found myself a small flat above a firm of undertakers in the main street. The so-called office turned out to be just an empty room on the first floor of the house. To start with there was just a phone on top of an old orange box, but it was quite sufficient for me and I settled in quickly, making contact with every possible news source in town.

Gerry on our trusty Lambretta which got us all around the Cotswolds when I was working on the Gloucestershire Echo

Gerry had decided to follow me and got herself a good job running the electricity board show room in Winchcombe, just outside Cheltenham. I had bought myself a Lambretta motor-scooter, which could just about climb Winchcombe Hill carrying one of us while the other pushed, but it got us wherever we wanted to go. That first six months went fast and I did well in competition with other local papers, with some freelancing on the side. The newspaper then acquired a proper office in the High Street, with an assistant to handle advertising. We were moving up in the world.

Every time I found a story which I felt had national interest I sent it to the Daily Mail in Manchester, which was where I eventually wanted to be. It didn't please my competitors on other local papers, waking up to find a story they knew nothing about from their patch appearing in a national daily. One reporter who was also a stringer for the Daily Express, the Mail's arch rival, became so upset that he threatened to settle the score; but he never quite managed. I thrived on that sort of competition, needing a few scoops to stand me in good stead with the Daily Mail and welcoming the extra cash they brought in.

One morning a letter came from my boss in Cheltenham asking me to let him have my birth certificate. Now I had reached the age of 25, he said, I was eligible to join the newspaper's pension scheme. I had no alternative but to send it and face the music when the truth was known about my age. The avuncular Mr Hollinshead spoke plainly; 'I am so sorry that our relationship began with a lie...a great disappointment...what do you have to say for yourself?' It seemed as though I was about to be fired.

I took off my horn-rimmed spectacles with some relief and handed them to him. 'Have a look at those,' I said.

He put them to his face and pronounced, 'They just have plain glass'.

I then told him about the number of times I had been rejected because I didn't have enough experience for an evening paper. The old Catch 22 situation had to be dealt with somehow and the heavy glasses had succeeded in making made me look older.

'I'm sorry I lied about my age,' I told him, quite sure by now that he was going to get rid of me. 'To be honest, if I was put in that situation again, I'd probably do the same, unless a better idea occurred to me.'

To my surprise he was more than understanding. He reviewed my work over the past six months and told me how pleased everyone was with the results from the Evesham office and how much the readership had improved. 'We will wipe the slate clean,' he said. 'No more lies. You can get rid of those damned glasses: this time, you can keep your job and I'll pay you as though you were twenty-five.' I never expected that. I could have kissed him. I still have those horn-rimmed specs tucked away in a drawer somewhere.

Those were happy days in Evesham, scooting about the Cotswolds with Gerry, spinning stories about life in the gentle hills, amongst the timeless thatchers and weavers, the huntsman and their hounds, hearing their scandals some of which occasionally made it to the pages of the Daily Mail. By now it was time to experience the pressures of a bigger paper and I took an opening on the Birmingham Post and Mail. The Post was the morning paper; the Mail came out in the evening, which meant tight deadlines in Britain's second city, growing daily with an influx of Asian and West Indian immigrants. It was here that I finished the NUJ's training scheme, the most valuable part of which was 'Essential Law for Journalists', ending with an exam invigilated at Birmingham University, the nearest I ever got to higher education. But, for what it's worth, no employer has ever asked me anything about it. In those days they were only interested in your track record.

The Post and the Mail were straight, down-to-earth papers, which knew their readership and served them well, even though the city was culturally and ethnically diverse. Its was a very busy life serving two news desks, two sets of sub-editors, each with a claim on your time and what you were doing. I had to get onto a story quickly and write fast and could expect to be covering four or five stories in a day. That was certainly the case when I was sent to run their Coventry office for a while: I would rarely finish work before midnight.

I shared a flat with a reporter from the Coventry Evening Telegraph, but it was a short-lived friendship because his paper was in competition with mine and he didn't like being scooped: who does? He expected me to tell him what stories I was following so he wouldn't be embarrassed, but that was never going to happen so far as I was concerned.

One Friday evening I got a call from Ken Donlan, the news editor of the Daily Mail in Manchester. He said that if I could get there by Monday morning he would offer me a job as a reporter: words magic to my ears! But what about the Post & Mail? I enjoyed working for them and I was supposed to give them a month's notice, so I explained my predicament to the editor in Birmingham, who couldn't have been more under-standing. At first he asked whether I'd been attracted by the

41

salary the Daily Mail was offering. I had to tell him, quite honestly, that I had completely forgotten to inquire about pay. That was the way it was with me. I knew where I needed to be. The money came second. No wonder someone once told me I'd never get rich being a journalist. The editor, a seasoned journalist himself, then said, 'Officially you are supposed to work out your notice but opportunity rarely knocks twice, so go and the best of luck to you.' Over that weekend I packed my only suitcase, tied, it to the back of my scooter and set off for Manchester in search of digs.

Back then, the Daily Mail was a reputable broadsheet with a strong team of well-known journalists headed by Harold Pendlebury, the doyen of Northern reporters. There was also strong southern Irish contingent... Clancy, Dempsey, Donlan, O'Flaherty, Mulchrone...who could all write well and charm their way out of any awkward situation, but they were tough too and I learnt to be careful not to upset them if I was in opposition on a story. Manchester was full of reporters who had learned their trade the hard way and always under constant pressure from their news desks not to miss any important detail of a story.

All the national dailies and Sunday papers were printed in Manchester and the competition between them was deadly. Sometimes the stories reporters were sent to cover were not that exciting, even a murder or a kidnapping could be pretty run of the mill unless a good angle came up. The tactics needed to stay ahead of the game were often more interesting than the actual stories and on the Mail, if I didn't make the best of the story when it came to the writing, I'd have to rewrite it and keep on re-writing until the news-editor was satisfied.

When I first joined the ranks of the Daily Mail, the youngest reporter on a Northern daily at the time, I was made to write one of my early stories several times before it was considered to be acceptable. It was a piece I had to put together about a fire at a public school, gleaned on the telephone one evening.

On 6th February 1958, Harold Pendlebury answered a phone in the newsroom to hear the faltering voice of photographer Peter Howard in a state of shock. He was calling from a phone box at Munich airport. The plane on which he was travelling with the Manchester United football team had just crashed on take-off in thick snow and burst into flames. Peter had been hurled out of the open side of the plane still in his seat and had landed on the runway, uninjured.

Harold immediate realised that he was listening to the story of a miraculous escape and that this call was probably the first news of the crash. So he gently coaxed Peter to keep talking and to give him an unique eye witness account not of just what had happening but a running commentary of the drama unfolding before his eyes. From the phone box, Peter was watching rescuers desperately trying to help people out of the flaming wreckage. Harold managed to keep the photographer talking for perhaps half an hour, calmly feeding him questions until he had all the detail he needed for a front page story that plunged Manchester into mourning. In that crash twenty-three people died, including eight star players, killing practically the whole team. Peter Howard was back in the air again weeks later taking aerial pictures to help him regain his confidence after that terrible shock.

Disasters of any kind are awful events to cover, especially if the wives, children, girlfriends and relations of those missing face agonising days and nights waiting for news, as can happen with disasters below ground or in the air. Those terrible vigils, such as coal mine accidents or aircraft disappearances, bring out the best and worst in people.

At a coal mine tragedy in Yorkshire, where miners were trapped underground by a roof collapse, I was waiting at the pithead with a large group of relatives when I noticed that one young woman in a shawl stood aside from the rest. It turned out that she was having an affair with one of the men still trapped in the mine. Waiting not far away was the miner's wife. I was left wondering how that scenario might have played itself out: the young woman decided to leave the scene after a while, but I never followed up. The miner was brought out alive on a stretcher in the early hours and was accompanied to hospital by his wife.

One Sunday evening Harold Pendlebury and I were called out to head for Castleton, an ancient village tucked away in the Peak District of Derbyshire, where rescuers were searching for a young man who had disappeared into one of the caves. These hills are honeycombed with old lead mines pre-dating the Romans. The caves can descend five hundred feet below ground to rivers flowing through the earth's core: the real stuff of legend.

Neil Moss, a twenty-year-old Oxford undergraduate, had joined members of the British Speleological Association to explore the known limits of Peak Cavern. When we got there, caving experts from within the community were assembled at the huge gaping mouth of the cave with all the rescue kit they thought they would need, but the early signs were that it was going to be an especially difficult operation. The explorers had decided to investigate a newly-discovered fissure deep below ground.

Only a hundred feet or so down, the temperature plunged and it was very cold, very wet and very dark. I found it hard to imagine what the conditions must be like a lot further down. We were told that access to the route the expedition had taken was hazardous. The pot-holers had to squeeze down steep narrow passageways which flooded after rain. There was one long stretch, which was barely high enough for men to crawl along, leading to a further gap through which they had to slide on their bellies. At the end that ordeal they were faced with thigh high icy water, in a muddy pool leading to yet another tiny opening, through which it was only just possible to squeeze a human body. By then, the expedition would still have only reached the fissure they had to explore.

An alloy ladder had been dropped into a narrow, tubular, opening and Neil Moss had clambered on to it, slithering his way down into the unknown. The party thought that the narrowness of this opening would prevent him from sliding all the way down, but he had encountered a corkscrew twist in which he became wedged so that he could not move at all. A light line was lowered to him, but it snapped three times.

There was talk of sending a Navy frogman down to the river below to try to push Neil up, but that seemed such an impossible feat: how could he possibly find the right hole for a start? Anyway, as far as I know, it never happened. There was even talk of fetching a superhuman midget from a circus who would be lowered down the tube upside down to attach a line to the student, but I don't know if such a nightmarish rescue bid was ever attempted. The very thought of it made my skin creep and I made me wonder if it might be a wild idea concocted by one of the Sunday tabloids.

For some hours Neil Moss had been able to talk to his rescuers, albeit with difficulty, but his body had remained wedged tight in the fissure. At this point the build-up of carbon dioxide made him lose consciousness. Despite valiant attempts to rescue him throughout the following day his body remained stuck just below the corkscrew in the hole until, finally, he was pronounced to be dead. His father, anxious that no further lives be endangered trying to rescue him, requested that his son should be allowed to remain undisturbed and that the fissure be permanently sealed.

When all the rescuers and villagers had gone, an eerie silence descended over the hillside. I went to the parish church to ask the vicar if he would like to come with me to the deserted cave entrance to say a prayer. He thought it was appropriate. I thought so too, but more than that I could see it would make a fitting end to such a tragic story. My photographer's shot of the vicar in his white cassock, his arms spread out in front of the mouth of the cave, made the front page of the Daily Mail the next morning. At the very moment the picture was taken a white owl, its huge wings fanned out, flew from the cave directly above the vicar. Down below, in the village pub where other reporters were filing their own stories unaware of where I had been, I quietly told Harold Pendlebury about the picture that was now on its way back to the office.

There was great spirit of camaraderie in the newspaper world which made me feel as if I was part of a big family, although there has to be one person, I suppose, who's always going to betray your trust. It happened to me on what was my first big story for a national newspaper. In 1958, Donald Campbell was attempting to break his own water speed record on Lake Coniston. Gerry and I had recently got married and she came with me. We were only up there about a week when Campbell plumed across the lake in Bluebird K7 to set a new world record of 248 mph. I had done a long interview with Campbell and was going through my notes when Daily Mail reporter, Ben Jordan, who had driven up from Manchester to get in on the story, asked if he could help me.

He had managed to get a line to the office on one of the few phones in the hotel and suggested that if I sat down and wrote the story I could hand it to him page by page and he would file it for me. He was supposed to be a colleague, so why not, I thought. When I'd finished we went for a drink. I was looking forward to seeing the story in print, knowing it would be given a big spread with all the pictures. The next morning the newspaper arrived and indeed the story got a terrific show... but with Ben Jordan's by-line...no mention of me at all. It was a huge disappointment. When I banged on Jordan's hotel room door, demanding to know why he'd done such a thing he just said: 'You've got to look after Number One in this game mate.'

I told him he'd made a big mistake. He might forget all about it, but I would not. One day, maybe years down the line, the score would be settled. Gerry was livid with him, knowing what the story had meant to me. That night, at a fancy-dress party thrown by Lady Campbell at the hotel to celebrate her son's new world record run, Gerry lost her temper with the odious Ben Jordan. He'd made some smart-arse remark and she gave him a left hook right on the point of his jaw. He had come to the fancy dress party in a St. Trinian's girl's gym-slip. Gerry was a cuddly, innocent figure in pyjamas, carrying a teddy bear. Suddenly, wallop. Jordan's feet left the ground and he fell flat on his backside. He sat there, with his skirt up round his waist, looking totally shocked. He stayed down too, clearly dazed, until he recovered his senses and left the party. How was he to know that Gerry was left-handed, very strong and packed such a powerful punch. Fleet Street colleagues around him jeered and they never let him forget that night.

The news editor spotted that something had gone awry on the Coniston story, from the style in which it was written and made sure that Jordan and I wouldn't cross paths for a long time.

CHAPTER 6

THE EMERALD ISLE

In the Spring of 1959, Gerry and I were posted to Dublin from where I was supposed to cover the twenty-six counties of the Irish Republic. My Irish friends in the office had told me to regard it as a foreign country and cautioned me that being English, I should avoid lecturing the locals on how to live their lives. Good advice. I gained a reputation of being more Irish than the Irish, revelling in their great good humour and their sometimes wonderful lack of logic.

Approaching June and the start of the holiday season, I noticed a paragraph in an Irish Tourist Board's magazine announcing that a particular bay on the west coast would be closed to tourists for the season, with no explanation given. I remarked to Gerry that there had to be a story there. My first call was to the local Garda station where a sergeant told me that the beach was to be closed because 'the lady with the blonde hair was back.'

'So, what's wrong with her?' I asked.

'Ah! Well, the last time she was sighted in these parts' the sergeant replied in a broad west coast brogue, 'there was a whole spate of unexplained deaths along the coastline'.

For a second I thought I was on to a mass murder of some kind. I asked him if he had seen this lady himself.

'I have so. On the rocks this very mornin'. She was siting' by the edge of a natural pool down there…very popular for swimming.' I couldn't see where this was leading so I asked him what she looked like.

She had the long blonde hair down to her waist,' said the sergeant.

'So, did you talk to her?' I asked him.

'I did not, she was gone in a flash with one flip of the tail fin, back into the water and away'. Naively I thought this was just a joke.

It sounds as though you're talking about a mermaid, I said. Quite unfazed, he confirmed that he was indeed talking about the mermaid. I asked him if anyone else had seen this apparition and he happily gave me the numbers of a local schoolmaster and a parish councillor. I spoke to them both and they too were quite sure they'd seen a mermaid, with tail flaying in the water. I asked if this fishy femme fatale was a young mermaid, or was she getting on in years, because the police sergeant had said it was forty years ago that she last appeared. They thought she was young, but they were not close enough to be quite sure!

I wondered why they hadn't gone down to the beach to make certain that they were seeing straight. Could the mermaid they thought they had seen be the daughter of the original one? I mean, if she was the one who last appeared four decades ago, she might be a little grey-haired by now. Anyhow, why did they think this mermaid, regardless of whether she was the daughter, the mother, or the great aunt, have anything to do with the drownings on that part of the beach? I should have bitten my tongue and kept these queries to myself, just making sure that indeed there had been several drownings in the area over the years, but there was nothing on record of anything suspicious.

None of the three had any answers to these obvious questions but they were not to be moved. They stuck to what they imagined they had seen and did not take at all kindly to being ridiculed by a foreigner. I needed to understand that strange things happen in the countryside, strange and even para-normal events: mermaids in their part of world were long considered to be a portent of impending bad luck. Because of that the beach would stay closed. End of the matter. Fair enough. This was the west of Ireland, the land of the little people, not the east or west coast of England.

The Land of the Little People. This was the 'silly season' when the Dail, the Irish Parliament, was in recess and there wasn't a lot of hard news about. So why not try writing a funny, tongue-in-cheek piece for the news-desk in Manchester? About half-an-hour after I'd filed the story. I got a call from the night editor, Jimmy Lewthwaite, a no-nonsense, hard-headed Lancastrian, who basically wanted to know if I'd taken leave of my senses.

'I can't run this load of old bollocks. I haven't seen it running on any of the tapes.'

I decided to give the story to a colleague in Dublin, Tony Gallagher, who worked for the Press Association: he checked it out for himself . Being Irish he wasn't in the least surprised to learn of mermaids in the west of Ireland and filed his version of the story. Now my story had got to the Press Association it had to be true, but not to Jimmy Lewthwaite. He wasn't having any of it. 'You'll be telling me a leprechaun is running for President next', he said. That was the end of my dalliance with mermaids... the one that got away. It never reached print in any paper as far as we could discover, but it stuck in Jimmy Lewthwaite's mind. Any time he was on duty when I was filing a story from Dublin, he would call out to make sure there were no bloody mermaids in it.

One quiet morning in Dublin, there was to be the official unveiling by the Mayor of a statue at the River Liffey end of O'Connell Street. Jimmy was on duty again but was not interested in such an ordinary event, so I wandered along to watch anyway. A brass band was playing as the shroud was pulled away, only to reveal a young boy peeing into the water below, but all that came out was a little trickle, to shrieks of laughter. Suddenly a lump of the newly laid turf surrounding the statue was hurled at one of the bandsmen and a fight broke out. In the melee the statue was torn from its platform and hurled into the Liffey. The morning ended with frogmen having to rescue it from the incoming tide. I wrote another tongue-in-cheek story, just a few paragraphs, but waited a while before sending it. Sure enough. Jimmy Lewthwaite was soon on the line.

'What about this nonsense in the Liffey, old man? It's on PA. I told him I was sending my piece on it right away. A few minutes later back came his reply. 'Where are the mermaids?'

The wonderful thing about working in Ireland as a journalist is that events can change in an instant and you must always be prepared for the unexpected. If you ask someone the directions to somewhere, don't be surprised if they tell you: 'If I was going there, I wouldn't start from here.'

One weekend an American film, 'Darby O'Gill and the Little People', made in 1959 and starring a young Sean Connery and Janet Munro was to be given its premiere, with a showing in Dublin. It was a fantasy about leprechauns, directed by Robert Stevenson. The special effects were good but the acting mediocre. Nevertheless, Hollywood decided to give it an impressive launch and invited some of its top movie stars to Dublin for that weekend, including Kirk Douglas, Robert Mitchum, Susan Hayward and Rita Hayworth ...all friends of the director John Huston who had a holiday home in Ireland.

The news-editor in Manchester decided I should try to arrange interviews with as many of these stars as possible, so as to write a full-page diary piece with pictures. Fine, except that the Hollywood PR had already organised their own photo-call in a special suite where they were knocking back champagne. No journalists were to be allowed in: the photographer had his pictures, but I had no story.

I sat at the hotel bar downstairs for quite a while, trying to pluck up the courage to gate-crash Hollywood's big party. What if it went horribly wrong and I was thrown out. That wouldn't go down too well with my boss in Manchester, or his even bigger bosses in London. I was feeling really dejected, not to be able to get anywhere near all these icons of the cinema when a tall distinguished looking man, with an American accent, came up next to me and asked the bartender for a pack of cigarettes. I had no idea who he was, but he asked me if I was alright. I must have looked as though I had the weight of the world on my shoulders. I told him I was basically in the shit and for why. My boss would probably kill me. He smiled and said, holding out his hand,

'Maybe I can help you? My name's Walt Disney.'

His name rang in my ears and it was as though I'd just met the King. He took me upstairs and almost immediately the crème de la crème of Hollywood started to gather round. He introduced me as 'my young friend here' and more or less directed them to talk to me, saying, 'He wants to write something nice about you and what's brought you all over here'. Fortunately they were all in a good mood and since the prophet had spoken, happy to oblige. There I was talking to some of my screen heroes about the Emerald Isle and its Little People. Off the cuff chatter really. Who cares if Rita Hayworth believed in fairies... but coming from stars of their standing I had plenty to fill the diary column. Thank you. Mr Disney.

I loved working in the Republic, it suited my temperament and even my writing improved. The Irish have a great way with words and a talent for putting a really big story in perspective with a few chosen phrases. Their lack of any sense of urgency was a constant source of irritation to news editors back in England. Where else could politicians take a weekend off in the middle of a Presidential election and disappear from Friday till

50

Tuesday, leaving news of votes on important issues hanging in limbo? They'd just laugh it off saying that they weren't there to be at the beck and call of the English. No-one seemed that bothered when the best laid plans came unstuck. I once went all the way to Limerick from Dublin to do a colour piece on the wedding of an Irish aristocrat. The photographer, Charlie Fennell, didn't realise until he got back to the office that evening, that he had no film in his camera, rendering the whole operation a complete waste of time.

One day, covering the Irish Horse Show at Ballsbridge, Fennell was supposed to take a picture of a Lady Melissa somebody-or-other inspecting her favourite horse. The only other human in the stables, on the other side of the horse, was a dishevelled looking woman with a bucket and mop. Click, Charlie took his picture. The next morning's paper carried a lovely a shot, not of Lady Melissa, but of the stable girl. The caption read: 'Lady Melissa…with her horse Fennell.' Fennell was the name of the photographer not the horse. I have no idea how the mix-up came about, but no-one was particularly concerned, least of all Lady Melissa who, at the time, was the subject of the latest scandal involving the wayward Irish aristocracy. The stable lass's social standing sky-rocketed that day.

There was never a dull moment. Irish films were drastically cut by the bishops who formed the Board of Censors and who let nothing pass if they thought it might lead their flock astray. Behind the scenes all the bishops turned up every week or so to enjoy the suspect movies before doing their hatchet job.

I was sorry to leave Dublin and move back to England after only six months. Gerry was pregnant with our first baby, Jane. For a while, I worked for the paper from her parent's home in Stoke-on-Trent.

CHAPTER 7

BREAKING THE RING

The news editor posted me to Sheffield with the job of breaking up the cosy ring that operated among the national daily reporters, who wanted a quiet life and shared the stories they were going to cover each day. That way nobody was ever scooped. The editor wanted all that to change.

Gerry and I bought our first house in Totley, a quiet residential area north of the city. It was a nice, three-bedroom, semi-detached house with apple trees growing in the garden, costing some £2,400, with a ten percent deposit. Our first-born, Jane, spent her early childhood there and our second child, John, was born in the same house.

I'll never forget that night. We had returned from a party about midnight when Gerry went into labour. As she lay on the bed upstairs, I started to spread old newspapers around the floor, expecting there to be a lot of blood and to put pans of water on to boil. I'd seen someone doing that in an old film. I rolled up a towel and handed it to Gerry to bite on. She smiled at all my antics and said, 'What do you think this is, the Crimea?' John popped out without a problem, just as the midwife arrived. Gerry was enjoying tea and toast about ten minutes after the birth.

It was my good fortune to meet Allan Kassell in Sheffield, a freelance journalist who became another life-long friend. He and his partner ran the South Yorkshire News Agency which covered for all the national dailies printed in Manchester. He kindly kept me abreast of what the competition was doing and seemed to enjoy my stirring things up a bit by being the lone ranger. My area was vast: Yorkshire, Lincolnshire, Stafford-shire and Nottinghamshire, which meant a lot of driving to follow up stories. I'd have so many possible stories in the pipeline, awaiting some dramatic development, that it was time-consuming to keep abreast of them all. Sometimes hunches paid off, sometimes they didn't. I would even write to people in jail on remand, awaiting a court hearing, to learn more about their story so as to get the edge on my competitors.

There was one crook, Lawrence Moorby. According to a local paper, he had strolled into a police station one night and confessed to a string of crimes committed years earlier but there were no other details. In an exchange of letters with him, from Lincoln prison, he told me about his lavish lifestyle, posing as a rich company director, forging stolen cheques all over the north of England. He had lived it up until the police were getting too close and then he fled to the continent to join the French Foreign Legion. As a legionnaire he had spent four years in one horrific battle after another fighting against marauding Arab tribes, until he couldn't take it anymore and deserted. I told him that because he had returned to England and given himself up he might be given a suspended sentence. I would meet him at the court when he walked free and take him to a hotel to write his story. The deal was that he would talk to me exclusively and would not utter one word to any others pressuring him outside the court.

Allan Kassell, journalist and film producer, and one of my lifelong friends from Yorkshire; also the best man at my wedding with Rowena

We had quite a good relationship by then and he agreed.

On the day of the hearing the Grimsby magistrates did let him off with a suspended sentence and he walked out into a clamouring posse of my competitors, but he shoved his way through and made a bee-line for me. Within seconds we were in my car and away at speed. It worked well. For weeks my competitors on other papers did their best to even up the score, but over a year I managed to finish up ahead. As a result our arch rival, The Daily Express, asked me to join their paper for a lot more money. I turned down their offer out of loyalty: days later the Daily Mail announced that they were sending me to the Fleet Street Mecca.

The Street of Ink, as it still was in the early sixties, made me feel as though I was part of something very powerful; it was exhilarating just to walk down Fleet Street, between the headquarters of the great newspapers of the day, in which tomorrow's headlines were being pounded out and upon which even governments could fall. No wonder they called the press, the media, 'The Fourth Estate.' Oscar Wilde once wrote that the press had become the only estate to have eaten up the other three: there certainly were days when there seemed to be some truth in that, listening to veteran journalists planning their next investigations into some MP, Minister or Peer of the Realm. The two big press barons, Northcliffe and Beaverbrook, behaved as though the fate of the nation lay in their hands. Each newspaper was like a powerhouse: just being in its embrace gave you that feeling you were part of something important, yet somehow menacing. It had first claim on your time and effort.

Each newspaper had its favourite pub and at ten o'clock every morning the Mail would hold its first meeting in a back bar to discuss stories worth considering for that day. When I arrived for my first day in the Fleet Street office, just before ten in the morning, the newsroom was deserted. One of the secretaries told me to hurry round to the pub if I didn't want to miss what was going on. As I arrived, just in time, the news-editor nodded his approval.

The drill, in those days, was that newcomers would be on the day shift for a few weeks to get a feel for the way the paper worked and then were assigned to the 'dog watch', seven pm until four am, when the last edition rolled off the presses. It was up to newcomers to work their way off that list by coming up with a few stories, preferably exclusive, that would at least make page leads, if not the splash. At night, following up a story might take you all over London, from the high spots to some of the lowest dives in town, from east to west, but wherever you went it was invariably going to involve a lot of booze. It was difficult not to become part of the drinking culture. So many of the contacts needing to be nurtured, especially in the police force and legal profession, who expected you to be generous with your hospitality: if you didn't drink, then there was something wrong with you. From its beginning as a printing centre, Fleet Street had always been fuelled by ink and alcohol. Drinking was round the clock. At dawn the Press Club would still be heaving with reporters and sub-editors and their contacts, all shrouded in smoke. Sometimes I would roll home at about six or seven for breakfast and some sleep before starting the process all over again. It required a lot of stamina to keep up the pace.

I eventually got myself off that gruelling night shift by suggesting a story about a German made drug, Thalidomide, which was causing deformities in new-born babies. It was marketed in the late nineteen fifties as a treatment for morning sickness, with disastrous consequences. An American woman, Mrs Sherri Finkbine, who was three months pregnant and had been taking the drug, was refused permission for a legal abortion by her home state of Arizona. She needed to have the operation within a week and at that time the only place in the world where she could have it done legally was Stockholm. The Swedish medical board agreed, provided she came immediately.

I went home from the night shift with the story still in my pocket because it came in too late to run it in our last edition. I had breakfast, packed my passport and a bag and returned to the office in time for the morning meeting. The news editor on the day shift, Jimmy Anderson, hadn't realised that I was on nights, so when I suggested flying to Stockholm on the next plane to cover this important new test case his eyes lit up and he gave me the go-ahead. By early evening I was in Sweden: to hell with the dog watch. The night news-editor was not pleased when I didn't turn up for my shift, but there was nothing he could do about it. I did telephone him from Stockholm to apologise. He called me a cheeky sod, but he seemed to understand. When I returned to London, making two big by-lined features out of the story, he put me straight back on the dog watch as a lesson. Luckily it was only a couple of nights before I was freed again.

An amazing aspect of Fleet Street's drinking culture was that some journalists could drink as though it was going out of fashion, but still write a decent story, although filing it over the phone to a copytaker, as was the custom in those days, may not have always sounded too coherent. I could never do that; drink just muddled my thoughts and I couldn't bear the idea of turning in copy which I knew to be rubbish. I made a rule: finish the work first, then have a drink. Even so, I only managed to get by in Fleet Street by sticking mostly to beer: whenever I drank spirits, especially Scotch, I certainly wouldn't feel like work:

sometimes work and play ran dangerously close.

I went to Davos to cover Lord Snowdon's Swiss skiing holiday where Princess Margaret had flown out to meet him. From the moment she arrived the French and Italian paparazzi wouldn't leave her alone: they wanted shots of her in action on the ski slopes and even better taking a tumble at some point, but she was in no sporting mood. The local police chief, Florian Meier, only had four uniformed policemen to help him control dozens of clamouring photographers. He hadn't got a chance, while Princess Margaret was becoming more and more angry, threatening to cancel the trip and go home. Nevertheless, she did co-operate with a small group of English photographers, some of whom she knew. They eagerly agreed to conspire against the paparazzi. Once the Snowdons were safely inside their holiday chalet, the real fun started.

Over the next few days, they sent the paparazzi on wild goose chases all over the Alps, giving the Princess a chance to escape for a few hours. She never did take to the ski slopes, unlike her husband. One afternoon, while he distracted the paparazzi, we went with Her Highness to a very exclusive little alpine hotel, the Chesa Grischuna in Klosters, where there was a cosy bar and a nine-pin bowling alley. The Princess, it turned out, liked bowls and was pretty good at it. She also liked a large gin and tonic or two. I joined her, with a double Scotch on the rocks. We played bowls, got some good pictures and everyone was happy.

CHAPTER 8

THE PAINTED SHIP

Christmas always seems to be a time for disasters, somewhere in the world. On 22nd December, 1963, I was ready to settle down with the family and enjoy the festivities when a call came from the news desk to tell me that a Greek-owned cruise ship, the Lakonia, with 646 British and Irish passengers on board and 376 crew, had caught fire off the Canary Islands. A big rescue operation was underway: off you go.

With the first distress signals, the Lakonia's position was immediately fed into the computers of the Atlantic Merchant Vessel Emergency Reporting system, which plots the location, course and speed of some eight hundred and fifty merchant ships in the North Atlantic at any one time. The computer showed five vessels within a hundred miles of the Lakonia. The nearest one, the British tanker, Montcalm, was about half an hour away and had already changed course towards the blazing ship. The RAF in Gibraltar was on call and the US Air Force base at Lajes in the Azores was sending four C-54 rescue planes, carrying 42 life rafts, enough for six hundred people, together with four hundred blankets and six paramedics, who would jump into the water to help passengers. I was soon on a plane to Casablanca: Christmas was over before it had begun.

Aboard the Lakonia, the Christmas cruise had turned into a nightmare.

When passengers boarded at Southampton, the brochure in their cabins had read, 'Have your holiday with all risk eliminated … a holiday you will remember for the rest of your life.' Out in the Atlantic, passengers in the main lounge were enjoying a Tramps fancy dress ball and did not hear the alarm bells, as the fire raged below, people watching a Bob Hope movie in the cinema thought the bells were part of the film's plot: the ship's loudspeaker system wasn't working properly so no fire instructions were given. Just after midnight Captain Zarbis gave the order to abandon ship. The last SOS from the Lakonia read: 'I cannot stay any more in the wireless cabin. We are leaving the ship. Please help immediately.'

On deck, as the ship started to list, there was near anarchy. Greek officers were screaming contradictory instructions to each other, leaving crewmen bewildered. Some jumped overboard; some tried to free the lifeboats, but the davits were jammed solid on half of them. They had been freshly painted in a make-over before the cruise began, but no-one had checked to make sure they were all working properly.

Passengers, who could not understand what the Greek officers were saying, were left to organise themselves into groups and head for the muster points through the thickening smoke. Many of the passengers were dressed in pyjamas, night gowns, evening clothes and even in fancy dress costumes, completely unprepared for a sixty-foot drop into the Atlantic.

The water temperature was 64 degrees and the sea was calm, but even so some of the elderly passengers and small children were dead before they hit the waves. Others who jumped were strangled by improperly fitted life jackets. As dawn broke there were twenty ships, including the British aircraft carrier Centaur, overlooking a vast expanse of ocean scattered with countless bodies bobbing face down on the water. Rafts and lifeboats kept banging into the windward side of rescue ships and it took hours to haul the living and the dead aboard. British sailors on the first ship to arrive, the Montcalm, told me that when they realised some of the first men trying to climb aboard were members of the Lakonia's crew, they tossed them back into the sea, ordering them to fetch a passenger.

It was near midnight on Christmas Eve as I watched the Montcalm steer slowly, eerily, into harbour at Casablanca, an incongruous brightly-lit Christmas tree lashed to its main mast, its foredeck laden with dead bodies arranged in neat rows. The survivors stood aft, leaning silently on the rails, many of them still in shock. Sailors from the Montcalm told me their rescue stories. At the final count one hundred and twenty-eight people had died. Survivors said they were amazed the death toll hadn't been much higher, such was the chaos and lack of proper safety procedures aboard the ship.

Traveling abroad, at a moment's notice, takes its toll on family life. Fortunately. Gerry ran her own women's fashion business in Beaconsfield which kept her well occupied while the children were at school.

During the Paris riots and strikes of 1968, BBC TV News flew crews into France from a private airfield at Denham. One evening Gerry and I were enjoying a party at a friend's house when a neighbour rushed in, with a message from my office, saying I had to leave immediately. A plane was waiting for me at the Denham airfield. The hosts thought it was some kind of ruse to get me out of staying any longer at the party...until the next evening that is, when they saw me on the TV News reporting from the Rue Saint Germain as the armed branch of the French police charged down on rioting students. Sometime later, these same friends were enjoying a dinner out and happened to meet my news editor. They apparently told him what had happened, commenting that I always had some fanciful excuse for leaving social occasions early, usually claiming that my editor wanted me to dash off somewhere. He interrupted, saying: 'But it was me. I sent him!' After that my friends came to accept that I might really be here today and gone tomorrow. Gerry, amazingly, took it all in her stride and got on with her life.

Sometimes the distances we had to travel in order to get to the heart of a story were enormous. I once flew from London to New York, then to Miami to pick up an American freelance photographer and on to Buenos Aires, all in one trip, to cover the Argentine junta's brutality against dissidents: the Pheno-menon of the Disappeared, they called it, Los Desaparecidos. Within a few hours of arriving we were arrested trying to film the Naval Barracks in Buenos Aires and came close to having all the camera equipment smashed.

The foreign editor in London once phoned me in Caracas, Venezuela, to ask me if I could nip down to La Paz, in Bolivia, to look into a cocaine story. On his map it was only a couple of inches, so he thought it was a quick trip. In reality, it took me nearly two days on the rickety planes of local internal airlines with many stops and delays, as it found its way over the Amazon basin and across the Andes. The airport in La Paz stands at thirteen thousand feet above sea level and it takes a couple of days, even with the help of coca tea, to recover from altitude sickness. The Andean women in their bowler hats and many coloured multi-layered dresses, all loaded with baggage, march up the mountain roads as agile as goats. We westerners are out of breath after a few yards.

There are some 170 small airfields in Bolivia from which the drug gangs can fly their cocaine. Flying in with the police, on a cocaine 'factory' raid, poses a considerable risk of not coming back. On one occasion, the police helicopter and its so-called elite crime busting squad of twelve men never returned. No-one heard of them again. They might have been bought by the Bolivian cartel or more likely killed. One day, I was to interview a minister in La Paz, who had publicly vowed to crack down hard on a particular drug baron. Just before I left my hotel to see him I had a call from his office to say he had been assassinated the night before. Almost every day while I was in Bolivia, someone was murdered in the internal battles between old and new drug cartels. One drug baron, who had built a school and a sports stadium for villages in his area, made a public offer to fund the repayment of Bolivia's national debt out of the millions of dollars he had made from cocaine smuggling. He regarded himself as untouchable by the law.

CHAPTER 9

WELCOME TO AUNTIE

It was on the cards that I might be sent by the Daily Mail to the New York office, but out of the blue I received an invitation to go for an audition at the BBC. They wanted to strengthen their news operation with a few seasoned reporters from Fleet Street. I had never considered broadcasting and was going to ignore their letter, but my friend and mentor, Vincent Mulchrone, by now a leading feature writer in the London office, persuaded me that I should get another string to my bow. He prophesied that, in the not-too-distant future, Fleet Street would have to change and that some of the newspapers would disappear, like a pip from an orange. Fleet Street would be forced to bring its technology up to date if it was to survive in the burgeoning media world. Radio and most importantly television would be the driving forces. So, think twice, Mulchrone advised. Go and have a talk with them.

It felt strange walking into Broadcasting House, in Langham Place, with its endless narrow corridors, the workforce and its old-fashioned studios tucked away behind closed doors. Completely different to the open-plan hustle and bustle of a busy newspaper. There was a different language too. People used abbreviations when referring to someone's designation. I was going to be interviewed by HNE and possibly ENCA, who were responsible to the DG. Translated, that meant Home News

Myself on joining the BBC from Fleet Street in May 1964.

Editor, Editor of News and Current Affairs, reporting to the top dog, the Director General.

The building in which I found myself was to be known simply as BH. I was ushered into a small sound studio with a single microphone on the desk and given a type-written script to read. But first I had to unscramble the story, which was all out of order in terms of news importance. After that came a screen test, my first acquaintance with a TV camera, followed by the formal interview with HNE, The Home News Editor, Tom Maltby. It seemed to go well and he said he would get back to me when the recordings had been checked. I was invited back for a further chat with the amiable editor while being scrutinised by a couple of other nameless 'suits' from the news hierarchy, who just sat there, unsmiling. They had that quizzical look about them that made me feel as though I was of a different species. But a few days later I was offered a job as a reporter. By the end of the week, with a bit of nudging from Vincent Mulchrone, I had taken the plunge and said farewell to the Street of Ink, not at all sure that I had made the right decision. What could it be like working for an organisation that seemed to enjoy being known affectionately as Auntie?

The atmosphere inside BH in those days was so formal: everyone knew their place and didn't step out of line, rather like the civil service, I imagined. I was quickly informed that the Beeb was now great fun, not at all like it used to be under the founder, Lord Reith, who had even ruled that radio presenters wear bow-ties and dinner jackets when reading the news. He sacked a famous presenter who was found in flagrante delicto with a naked lady one night in a radio news studio. The presenter's colleagues had pleaded with Lord Reith, a strict Presbyterian minister, to change his mind because it would be such a loss to the BBC. He eventually relented and re-instated the man, on condition that 'he never again read the Epilogue'.

I was gradually introduced to something called an Fi-cord, basically a shoebox with a quarter-inch spool-to-spool tape recorder inside and easy to carry over the shoulder. It was our main piece of kit, covering easy stories around London for use on Radio Newsreel. Every piece that made the air was scrutinised at the end of each week by Tom Maltby, who would politely suggest how it might be improved. He was a great help. So was my father. When he heard my first radio broadcast, in a voice I had decided to gentrify with a slightly posh accent, he just remarked, 'Who the hell do you think you are?' That was the end of that. I went back to being myself, though over time a broadcasting style and voice to suit each individual develops of its own accord. This applied particularly to broadcasts on the World Service, for the benefit of people in far-flung places, maybe with a patchy signal. The sound has to be easy on the ear. Writing for radio is a special art, one that requires each broadcast to sound as if it was unscripted and addressed to one person only, that someone sitting at home. It has to hold each listener's imagination.

Once the powers that be felt I could be entrusted with some simple technology, I was introduced to the heavier more robust recorder, the Uher, which could withstand a lot of knocking about. I was to be given a foreign assignment, primarily for radio, but I would also take with me a small twin-turret Bell and Howell film camera, in case there was a chance to shoot a piece. 'Mute film and tape' they called it, for use in TV News. I was to practice with this camera for a few days using a light meter; all simple stuff, they said. I would need to get used to filming before leaving for the Congo, where a civil war was raging with thousands of orphaned children starving to death. I was to try to locate them and then to team up with people out there from the Save the Children Fund. It was the sort assignment that would be banned by the cameramen's union these days; the very thought of a reporter shooting film would have them out on strike.

In the sixties, conflict in the Congo had spread throughout the whole state following the granting of independence from Belgium. Some factions supported the ousted Prime Minister, Patrice Lamumba while others backed Moise Tshombe, leader of the rich mining area of Katanga who enjoyed the support and lucrative favours of the foreign mining companies. It was one of the world's main sources of cobalt, copper, diamonds, tin and gold. Tshombe wanted his territory to secede from the rest of the new republic. The starving and abandoned children had mostly gathered in the eastern province of Kivu. They were suffering from a protein deficiency, Kwashiorkor, which attacks the liver and eventually kills.

Once I arrived in the capital, Kinshasa, I called at the British Consulate to let them know what I was trying to do. They had no idea what the situation might be like in Kivu between the warring factions as nobody from the consulate had been there. I needed to reach Bukavu, the provincial capital, but it was over 2,000 miles away and all internal civil air traffic had been suspended. However I learned that UNICEF, the United Nations Save the Children Fund, were flying emergency food supplies into the eastern province by private cargo plane. I located one of the pilots at Kinshasa airport and begged him for a lift. Before we flew off, I had time for a decent meal at a restaurant in town, thinking that maybe it would probably be the last one for a while. The menu included strawberries from eastern Congo, which was renowned for them, but the waiter told me that because of the war none had been brought in.

It took hours to make the journey, following the Congo river as it threaded its way through dense jungle that seemed never ending, with no signs of habitation anywhere. I couldn't help thinking of Joseph Conrad's classic boat journey up the Congo in 'The Heart of Darkness' with its frightening images of entrapment in impenetrable greenery. What if the plane crashed in the middle of nowhere, who would find us?

The town of Bukavu stands on a hill on the shores of Lake Kivu, near the border with Rwanda and Burundi. For years it had been the centre of trading with East Africa and sanctuary for thousands of refugees fleeing conflicts in countries on its borders. Many of its buildings bore the bullet holes etched into its battle-scarred history. There was an air of decay about the place, a forgotten outpost from Belgium's colonial past.

In the sixties the Eastern Congo was in the throes of a bloody war between the Simbas, supporters of the overthrown Prime Minister Lamumba and the Congolese army, spearhead by battle-hardened mercenaries. There had been massacres, pillaging of villages, the destruction of crops and inevitably, starvation and disease. When I arrived it was estimated that about 20,000 children, displaced by the war, were somewhere in the deeply-forested Maniema area to the west of Bukavu. In the Victorian era when the journalist Henry Stanley passed this way during his famous search for Scottish explorer David Livingstone, the name Maniema was enough to cause many of his bearers to run away. It had frightening associations with cannibalism and sorcery.

Save the Children had a small team trying to organise the survival of all these youngsters, but the odds were heavily stacked against them. Under constant threat from marauding guerrilla groups the business of bringing in medical and food supplies was fraught with danger. At a mission station run by nuns I was introduced to the overseas director of Save the Children, who had flown out from London to oversee the rescue and rehabilitation operation. His name was Colonel Hawkins. Slowly, as we looked at each other, our memories going into overdrive, the past came into focus. We had last met at Maresfield Park Camp, HQ of the Intelligence Corps in Sussex, when I began my National Service. He had been the commanding officer. Since his retirement from the army he had served with Save the Children as its overseas director. So we teamed up.

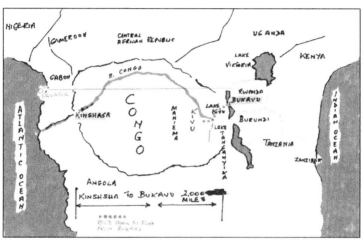

My first foreign assignment for the BBC – during the Congo's civil war of the mid-nineteen-sixties I made a 2,000-mile journey by air and road from Kinshasa to Bukavu in the eastern Kivu province to find Save the Children Fund nursing thousands of dying youngsters

The mission station stood on a hill overlooking a great plain which vanished into the darkness of the jungle. Word was to be sent to surrounding villages that children should make their way, as best they could, to the mission where there was food and help. There were no mobiles then and no telephone contact at all, so the messages were sent out the traditional way by local men on drums. They pounded out sequences every few minutes. Then, they said, it was just a matter of waiting as the sounds were picked up and sent on from village to village.

The basic little field hospital at Bukavu consisted of a long wooden building, with a waste channel running down the middle of the one primitive ward. Children hospitalised with Kwashiorkor were dying at a rate of six a day. Their hair would turn light orange as their skin broke into a rash of terrible sores. The destruction of crops and livestock by the Simba rebels had left villagers relying, for their survival, on grass and manioc, a tuber type of starchy vegetable of little or no protein value. Sometimes, when the children's hair turned orange, they would be cast out of their villages as witches. Traditional and primitive belief systems are strong in the Congo, though intertwined with Christianity. Sorcery, as for instance in Haiti and parts of Brazil, is common.

On our first foray into the forest, after several hours of bumpy travel along a single track, we came across the first signs of human life…a village of mud huts with grass-thatched roofs that hadn't seen a white face in a long time. We stopped the old jeep we had borrowed and were quickly surrounded by men women and children in ragged clothing. I put my Uher tape recorder on the bonnet to pick up all the noise and chatter and got to work with the film camera.

Suddenly, through a cloud of dust, emerged the splendid figure of a man in a feathered head-dress, his face, arms and legs painted white. I got him in focus as he walked and jumped towards us. What a great picture, I thought. I'll keep filming him until he walks past and then do a cutaway. Very technical for me. But, he didn't walk on. He stopped in front of the camera, leaping up and down and jabbering away like a mad parrot. Fortunately we were travelling with a UNICEF man who spoke the local language.

'He's very annoyed because he thinks you are stealing his spirit,' he said. Some time passed before our feathered friend, who turned out to be the local witch doctor, was persuaded that I meant no harm. I went to the tape recorder and pressed play. There was a great hush amongst the crowd when they heard the sound of themselves coming out of this little machine. The UNICEF man explained what 'magic' was going on. He produced a Polaroid camera, took a quick snapshot of the witchdoctor and showed it to him, explaining that the little gadget was simply giving him a present: a likeness of himself. There was no need to worry, his spirit would remain with him. The witch doctor smiled, showing everyone his picture. All was

66

well. The UNICEF man had one arm missing, which he said had been hacked off during a raid by the Simbas. They'd done it to free the evil spirits which, they had claimed, were residing in him.

Two days passed before the drum messages sent forth from the mission station produced a result. It was one of the most moving scenes I have seen, almost biblical. The nuns were ready with churns of powdered milk, made up that morning. Nurses had prepared beds in a large first aid tent, but it soon became alarmingly clear that this was not going to be anywhere near enough. Below the mission, winding its way out of the jungle and across the plain in an unbroken but jagged line, came ragged children of all ages, some so small they could barely be five or six, moving with difficulty through the rough grass; they had been on the move for a long, long time.

As they struggled up to the mission, my eye looking through the camera, caught sight of a little girl, perhaps eight years old, carrying a much smaller child, just a toddler. The girl was given a chair and sat down with the youngster, a little boy, on her lap; he looked so thin, his wide eyes dark and sunken. The nun poured the milk carefully into his mouth. He swallowed hardly a mouthful and the white liquid trickled down his chin. His eyes closed and a nurse came and gently took the child away wrapped in a towel. The little girl, his sister, silently followed.

Some of the children, who were recovering from the trauma of war and this disease, were taught to sing by the nuns. The higher grasslands of eastern Kivu has rich soil and can produce most types of fruit and vegetables but war throughout the sixties had ruined agricultural production. The nuns taught the children songs with lyrics that spoke about the crops that should be grown again to keep children healthy and strong. The choir they formed sounded so beautiful that Decca wanted to make a Christmas record. They'd heard the amazing voices in the radio documentary which I subsequently made ... Children of the Congo.

When I had finished my job in Kivu province I hitched a lift back to the capital the same way I had come in, on a UNICEF cargo plane, only this time it was empty. Right there, beside the airport in Bukavu was a market selling...strawberries. I bought a load and had them stacked in the empty plane. They sold in a flash at the market beside the airport back in the capital. Half the proceeds went to UNICEF and half to Save the Children and my camerawork turned out well enough to make a decent little TV News item on BBC 1. What more could a newcomer to Auntie ask for?

CHAPTER 10

LET THE PICTURES TELL THE STORY

After that trip, much of the sixties and seventies was packed with foreign assignments to trouble spots in Africa and the Middle East, including Israel, Cyprus and Aden, sometimes working for both radio and TV news at the same time, which can be very difficult. It imposes great restraints on how you use your time. The way reporters write for one medium is not the way they write for the other. Radio is more personal: a one-to-one relationship with someone listening at home or wherever they are. TV News scripts need to be written to complement whatever is being seen on the screen, not describe something you are watching unfold for yourself. So the writing is more like brush strokes in a painting, filling in any informational gaps not covered by what is being watched. If there is nothing to film, then the gap can be bridged by the reporter doing a 'piece-to-camera'. What is written for TV News, as a reporter, is governed by the footage that the cameraman has captured.

Picture this in your mind's eye: we are in Pamplona in northern Spain during the festival of San Fermin, when they have the running of the bulls through the street. Most of the audience are behind wooden barricades, except for macho, half-drunk young men waiting in the main square for a chance to play the matador for a second before they are sent flying. At a narrow neck in the street where the oncoming bulls are packed shoulder to shoulder a young man, wearing a red bandana, staggers drunkenly out of nowhere right into the way of this thunderous onslaught.

From where we are, at ground

BBC cameraman Richard Hill prepares to film the running of the bulls in Pamplona, northern Spain during the festival of San Fermin.

level, the cameraman, Richard Hill, is filming this man's sudden appearance. There are gasps because it looks as though he's going to be trampled to death. How can he possibly survive? He's being buffeted between tons of solid meat. Clouds of dust obscure him for a few seconds. We expect to see him lifeless, lying in shreds as the bulls rumble past, but as the dust clears the cameraman is back on him, somehow still standing. He reaches a doorway opposite, slowly slides down it, legs outstretched and falls fast asleep, still clutching a bottle.

The running of the bulls during the festival of San Fermin in Pamplona – a test of every young man's courage if he fancies being a matador for a few minutes

This amazing sequence is going to be the opening of my story. It tells you almost everything you need to know about the running of the bulls without any commentary. It's all about alcohol and danger. So, you let the audience watch the drama take its course, uninterrupted; all they want to know is whether this young man is going to live or die in the middle of this chaos. You say nothing until he reaches the doorway and the animals have gone. Only then, when the audience knows he's safe, do you begin your commentary and it must be brief; no time for facts and figures. You only have six seconds over which to say something before the man slides down the door and is out for the count. Opening lines, setting the tone of your whole story, can be difficult to find. Mine, in this instance, quite simply said 'During this dangerous week in Pamplona, if the bulls don't get you, the red wine will.'

CHAPTER 11

MURDER MILE

My introduction to the Middle East began with a baptism of fire. We had been trying for three days to get into Aden (now part of South Yemen) in the south of the Arabian Peninsula. The RAF airport at Khormaksar had been closed to commercial traffic because insurgents were now using Czechoslovak ground-to-air missiles. Myself and a TV News crew, Doug Smith and Keith Skinner, had travelled from Ethiopia to Djibouti, the nearest point to the Gulf of Aden. We persuaded an Indian pilot to fly us across the short stretch of water in his small plane which looked as though it had seen better days. He had been reluctant to make the journey. His only guide for the low-level flight was an old road map which he kept open on his lap as we made our way towards the coast. It took us maybe half-an-hour flying bumpily just above the waves before we touched down in complete darkness at Aden airport without even landing lights. Within half an hour we were in the street keeping our heads low, in a gunfight between insurgents and British troops.

Aden had been a Crown colony since 1937 – of strategic importance because it provided control of the entrance to the Red Sea. The region had been dogged by years of unrest, fuelled by Arab nationalism and anti-colonialism. Britain had decided to establish a permanent military garrison there in 1962 and increasingly married families and their children became targets as well as soldiers and some members of the press corps who were blacklisted by the insurgents from time to time. It was important every morning to check your vehicle carefully before climbing in and turning on the engine. And every evening, when I returned to my hotel room, I checked to make sure that someone hadn't tampered with the air conditioning system or the lavatory. That sort of thing became part of the way of life, like cleaning your teeth. Some journalists, usually American, liked to wear military-style clothing to make themselves look more battle-hardened on camera. A German TV reporter who dressed more like one of Rommel's desert tank commanders was shot dead as he walked from our hotel in the Crescent area to post a letter in the Arab marketplace. News vendors in

Beaconsfield where I lived at the time had posted a headline: 'TV reporter killed in Aden,' which caused Gerry some concern until the BBC reassured her that it wasn't me.

Insurgents had strongholds tucked away in the Radfan Mountains around Aden and a friend of mine, Colonel Brian Carter, then a lieutenant with the Royal Marines, 45 Commando, was on night patrol when they came under attack. They blasted away at elusive dark shapes and at dawn realised that the bombardment of rocks was coming from troops of angry baboons.

Press conferences called by the army or the British High Commission sometimes attracted large numbers and twice I noticed a strange face amongst us. Later I discovered that he was a member of the NLF, The National Liberation Front, posing as a reporter from some Arab news agency. I came to know him simply as Ahmed.

One morning during a street fight with British troops I had been crouching behind the remains of a stone wall to avoid incoming fire from a block of flats. When the shooting finally stopped and people came back onto the street soldiers set up road blocks in the hope of tracking down the snipers. I was in my car driving along Murder Mile – the Ma'alla Strait that headed to the port and a favourite stretch for snipers. The front passenger door was suddenly opened and in jumped my NLF "friend" Ahmed clutching a revolver. We were approaching a road block and he had spotted me from the crowd. He said: "I saw you hiding behind that wall this morning…I could easily have shot you."

I told him that if he didn't put his revolver out of sight immediately he'd be dead, and probably me along with him.

He put the gun under the seat, but only just in time. We had reached the road block. I wound down my window and showed the soldier my credentials. He looked at me and the man sitting next to me and I said we were on our way to a press conference. Amazingly, the young soldier waved us through. Ahmed now owed me a favour and gave me a contact number.

The violence in Aden during 1967 went from bad to worse. The British could no longer protect its bases or the married families living there and announced that it would be leaving the country sooner than anticipated. Most of the violence had been concentrated on Crater, the old Arab quarter of Aden built on top of a defunct volcano. British troops had tried to intercept arms and ammunition being smuggled into the area by the warring Arab factions but with little success. The Royal Northumberland Fusiliers had been responsible for 'policing' Crater but were driven out by insurgents with the loss of 22 soldiers. The Army High Command then announced that Crater would be a 'no go' area for British troops. But the Fusiliers were succeeded by the 1st Battalion, The Argyll and Sutherland Highlanders under Lt.-Colonel Colin Mitchell, known to everyone as "Mad Mitch." He decided to ignore the order to stay out of Crater and impose 'Argyll Law' instead. Spectacularly he led his troops into the teaming suburb with fixed bayonets and fifteen pipers playing 'Scotland the Brave.' The insurgents were taken by surprise. A few pockets of resistance were quickly silenced, and within 24 hours Crater fell strangely quiet, except for the haunting sound of 'The Barren Rocks of Aden' coming from a single piper poised on the roof of the bank. The Argylls were firmly in charge without the loss of any of their men.

The man in charge of all the forces, General Philip Tower, was fuming that his orders had been ignored and he made his feelings known at a press conference. An official from British High Commission branded "Mad Mitch" and his men "a bunch of thugs." There was a lot of real anger among rank and file soldiers in Aden over Colonel Mitchell's treatment. To them he was a hero, doing the job the way it should have been done. Regrettably, he was forced to resign his commission the following year, a victim of the higher political stakes being played out in Aden towards the end of yet another outpost of the British Empire.

Ideally Britain had wanted a peaceful end, leaving the framework for elections and a stable federal government. But the warring factions had different ideas. The NLF, The National Liberation Front, was a radical Marxist para-military organisation and a political party, not well disposed to Britain following the support given to Israel during the Six Day War with Egypt. They were well entrenched in Aden and had strongholds outside in the Radfan mountains. The other main group was FLOSY, The Front for the Liberation of South Yemen, which had received military aid from President Nasser of Egypt, until he was defeated by the Israelis. Neither side wanted to talk to the departing British because they didn't want to be seen in the wider Arab world as agents of colonial imperialism.

A very experienced negotiator, Lord Carrington, then First Lord of the Admiralty, quickly visited Aden, on a strictly unofficial 'fact-finding' mission. He approached myself and a journalist from The Times and asked us if we had any reliable way of contacting the NLF or FLOSY to arrange a meeting with him. It would have to be in a secure location and kept secret. As journalists we could not be present, nor could we expect any announcement from him when it was over. Reluctantly, we agreed. I called in my favour due from Ahmed of the NLF and The Times man had a contact with FLOSY. The meeting went ahead, in a 'safe' house in the Crescent area of Aden. We didn't really like acting as messengers for the British government, but it seemed to be for a good cause. Lord Carrington, at least, left Aden knowing that there would be trouble once the British had departed and that it was probably for the best to let the Arabs sort themselves out.

During those final weeks there was a great rush among the expats to sell any belongings they wouldn't be able to carry. They were forced to sell their cars, dirt cheap to the Arabs, and in some cases just abandoned them in the street. An RAF sergeant who refused to leave his prized mini for the Arabs had it lifted by helicopter and lowered onto the peak of a mountain. It stood there for a long time after the British had gone, out of reach, glistening brightly in the sun. The last Governor of Aden, Sir Humphrey Trevelyan left the country with no apparent successor. As a point of respect he had Government house repainted for whoever emerged victorious.

There was a week of bloodshed after the withdrawal and the National Liberation Front which had allied with the federal army were able to defeat FLOSY whose leaders fled the country. On seizing power the NLF established The People's Republic of South Yemen.

As a welcome break between troublespots, I was sent to cover the marriage of Jackie Kennedy to the Greek shipping magnate Aristotle Onassis – or try to cover it. The Press were barred from getting anywhere near it. It was held on the tiny island of Scorpios, which Onassis owned, off the east coast of Lefkas in the Ionian Sea. It had been five years since John F Kennedy's assassination in Dallas, Texas, and not everyone in American high society was happy that the President's widow was marrying a Greek with a past record for fraud, even though he was a billionaire.

After several hours of hard driving from Athens cameraman Bob Poole, sound recordist Barry Lanchester and I reached a coastal village, the nearest we could get to Onassis' private island. It was getting dark, there was nowhere to stay, and a villager suggested we borrow a rowing boat and make our way to a small yacht anchored in the bay. There was no-one on it and we could use it for the night. No-one seemed to know who owned it, or care for that matter, so we took up the invitation. The door to the cabins was not locked and soon we had a roof over our heads with plenty of room to stow all our equipment. The next morning, as we were working out how long it might take us to row all the way to Scorpios a small cruise liner flying an American flag came alongside.

The skipper was Greek. We shouted to him that we were a British TV crew trying to reach Scorpios to cover Jackie Kennedy's wedding. As soon as the Americans who had chartered the cruiser heard of our mission they became very excited and insisted that they take us. They were not going to miss the chance of gatecrashing such a special event. It was probably the highlight of their trip. Though it was a short journey to the island we realised that it would have been really hazardous in a rowing boat; even more so because Onassis had a private army who were firing rifles and flares at a flotilla of little Press boats trying their best to come ashore. It was chaotic.

On our cruiser, flying an American flag, we apparently had the right to sail anywhere in the Greek islands, and the skipper dropped anchor close to the Onassis yacht, Christina, named after his daughter who later inherited $500 million. The Americans on our boat were delighted because they had a great view of the wedding reception taking place below them. The Press boats were having a rough time though being kept at bay by the security guards. Some of the journalists toppled into the water.

The deck of our cruiser was so steady we were able to use a tripod to film everything. Barry, who took over the camera on the tripod, got some wonderful shots of Jackie Onassis on a 10 to 1 zoom lens. No-one dared fire any shots or flares at a ship flying the American flag. It was a really successful operation. Our American friends, who by now were celebrating with their own 'wedding party', were more than happy to sail us back to our rowing boat. We air-freighted our precious film back to London from Athens feeling very pleased with ourselves. It had been a lot of enjoyable effort, but worthwhile.

Later, as we were about to drink a toast to our own success, word came from London. They were very sorry, but something terrible had happened. The whole of our filmed footage had been damaged in processing. An awful mistake, they said, but it was unusable. "Lost in soup," is the phrase they use to describe this kind of set-back. But it doesn't come close to covering the way you feel when it happens. We drowned our sorrows.

There are difficult and dangerous occasions when there is no film to capture the drama of the day, although there may still be a piece for radio. During my first stint covering the Biafra war in the late sixties I was based in Lagos, standing in for the well-established radio correspondent Angus McDermid, who had returned to the UK for medical treatment. I was planning a trip to the front line in the southern part of Nigeria. I had no TV crew at the time, but in the bar at the Federal Palace Hotel in Lagos, where most journalists stay, I met a freelance camera-man, Francois Lovat, from Paris. He was covering for NBC in America, but he had no reporter with him. I told him about my trip and we decided to team up. He had a huge car for all his kit, a Volvo, built like a tank. All I carried was my Uher tape recorder and a notebook.

We took off and were followed by half a dozen other foreign journalists. It required several hours for our convoy to reach the area around Warri where we had been told we might find the Federal soldiers. The journey was mostly on a single road through thick forest but suddenly we were approaching a village onto which mortar shells were being lobbed and there were running soldiers, wearing the shoulder flashes of the Biafran army. For us, it was the wrong side, we had somehow overshot the Federal positions. Francois turned the car round and we all sped back the way we had come, but by this time the Federal army had regrouped. When they saw us speeding towards them they thought we must be foreign mercenaries on some sort of kill or be killed mission.

They started firing at us. Francois' car took some hits but none fully penetrated the heavy doors. We all stopped, got out, hands in the air and Francois, being a gutsy little character, said to one of the soldiers: 'You're from the coconut trees, you idiot. We're on the same side!' Bloody Hell, I thought, this is not going to be good. The soldiers didn't understand a word. They looked wild and scared and their eyes were yellowish, as though they'd been smoking hemp for days. They ushered all of us to a ditch and lined us up, facing their automatic weapons. A sergeant was shouting at us.

It had all happened so quickly and the only thought in my head was....it looks like they might actually kill us. I looked down the row of journalists and noticed that one, in pale blue trousers, was peeing himself. Francois then whispered in my ear: 'If they're going give an order to fire, duck down, run like hell along the ditch and into the bush.' I hung onto that thought, clutching at straws really, because if they opened fire at such close range we wouldn't have stood much of a chance: they'd have shredded us. It was a slim hope and worth pondering on for a few seconds while my head took in our predicament.

In desperation I raised my hand and asked the sergeant if we could have a cigarette. He nodded and while I was saying a quick prayer and lighting up a fag, along with a few others standing in the ditch, there was the sound of an army vehicle approaching. A young officer stepped out demanding that the sergeant tell him what was going on. What a relief. We produced our papers which the officer read carefully and we explained how we had managed to be travelling in the wrong direction in our search for his infantry battalion. I was very happy to be taken, with the rest of our group, to battalion HQ for further questioning. Within about half an hour accreditation was cleared with the Defence Ministry and we were allowed to stay. I later heard that the screaming sergeant had been killed in a raid on a Biafran stronghold. There were no pictures of our close call earlier that day, although, I was lucky enough to be able to send a radio piece from the safety of the broadcasting station back in Lagos.

The two opposing leaders in the Biafran war, General Gowon, for the Federal side and Colonel Odumegwu Ojukwu in Biafra, were both trained in England. Each had a good idea how the other might marshal his troops, but on the ground in Nigeria during the Biafran war there was often complete chaos, with many of the soldiers poorly trained. I once saw a squad carrying out what was supposed to be a bayonet charge in single file. If someone had lobbed a grenade in front of them they would have been shish kebab. The Minister for Information in Lagos, Mr Dizu, was economical with the truth, to say the least. He accused me of spreading misinformation and I was deported from the country.

Six months later my superiors in London sent me back with a TV News crew. We expected some difficulties. Along with Bob Poole, a very experienced cameraman and his sound-recordist, Barry Lanchester, we were all put under house arrest in our hotel while Mr Dizu at the Ministry decided what to do. No hardship … we lounged by the pool until the call came to report to his office. I waited inside the Ministry for an hour and a half

BBC cameraman Barry Lanchester. It was Barry who calmly fixed our technical problem while filming a firing squad during the Biafra War. He was then a sound recordist working with cameraman Bob Poole.

beyond the appointed time. A secretary finally came out and announced. 'Mr. Dizu will see you now.' Unfortunately, I arrogantly asked if her boss could give me another five minutes to finish my crossword. She must have delivered the message verbatim. Seconds later the large frame of Mr. Dizu loomed forth from his office. He yelled at me, 'I keep you waiting for three days and now for an hour and a half and you, Englishman, have the cheek to ask me for another five minutes.' I tried to apologise, but I had overstepped the mark. He continued: 'You are the worst kind of Englishman. I want you out of Lagos immed-iately. Go away,' and stormed out.

I took Dizu's words literally. We left the hotel and bade

79

farewell to Lagos. In the car Bob had hired, we made the long journey south to the rivers area of Port Harcourt where fighting was reported. We were heading for the Federal division led by Sandhurst trained Colonel Benjamin Adekunle, whose ruthless tactics made him a controversial figure in the Federal army. They called him The Black Scorpion. His '3rd Infantry Division' didn't have the sensational ring about it that he would have liked, so he renamed it '3 Marine Commando' without formal approval from Army Headquarters. He seemed to be able to do whatever he wanted. The day before we arrived at his unit a young officer in his command had strangled a Biafran prisoner. Adekunle wanted to demonstrate to the media that there was strict discipline among his troops. We expected that the officer who had killed the prisoner would be tried by military court, but Adekunle announced that the officer was guilty and would be executed.

The speed of events then took us all by surprise. A firing squad was randomly selected. Usually, with a military firing squad one of the marksmen is given a blank bullet, ensuring that no-one in the group knows for sure which of them fired the fatal round. Bob first focussed his camera on the group of four soldiers as they took aim and were given the order to fire. Very slowly, as the guns went off, he panned along the lines of agitated troops standing watching. Finally the camera reached the tree where the blindfolded soldier stood, his head drooping down, but still alive. It was a few more minutes before he died. Only three bullets had hit their target. Finally, an officer marched out and shot the blindfolded man in the back of the head. It was not a sight that anyone would wish to see. I could have insisted that we not film the execution at all, but I don't believe that would have affected the outcome. The world's Press was there to report whatever happened. I had seen more gory footage than this sent from war zones. It was not up to me to censor content. That was up to the editors in London.

This incident lasted ten minutes: one roll of film. We shipped it back to BBC TV News that night. In those days we took the film to the British Airways dispatch office at the nearest airport, signed it in and got a weigh bill number to send to London with an arrival time. Overnight an agency reporter (Agence France Press, I believe) who had also witnessed the firing squad and had been standing quite near to me, filed a story giving the impression that a BBC producer had been directing the entire event. He inferred that the firing squad had been asked to hold on while the television crew dealt with a technical problem. It is true that I had asked the cameraman to wait while a problem with the battery leads was solved but that took the soundman, Barry Lanchester, only a couple of minutes. My comments had been directed quietly to my colleagues, no-one else. However a member of the BBC Board of Governors had seen the agency story and complained to the Editor of News. He wanted my neck on the block. Fortunately, I was rigorously defended by my editor and so I kept my job.

I was in trouble again though not long after, in 1968, when the editor of BBC TV News, Desmond Taylor, asked me to go with a cameraman, Chris Marlow, to the National Heart Hospital in Marylebone, where Fred West, Britain's first heart transplant patient was recovering. The only problem, Taylor said, was that the patient's wife had signed a contract with our competitors ITN, giving them an exclusive interview with her husband when he recovered consciousness. Taylor wanted me to check whether there was anything I could do to redress the balance. In Fleet Street, if a

BBC cameraman Chris Marlow who came with me to film Britain's first heart transplant patient Fred West as he woke from his operation.

news editor asks you to do something like this, he expects you to go to any lengths...so I took it that I was being given a free hand. At the hospital I learned that the operation on Mr West had gone according to plan and he was taking well to his new heart, but he was not expected to come round for several days. The ITN reporter staking out the hospital had gone for his lunch at a nearby pub. I figured I probably had forty-five minutes, maybe an hour to do something. I asked no-one's permission knowing that I would almost certainly be told to go away.

Chris Marlow and I went into the hospital, located Mr West's ward and spoke to the sister in charge, who was soon to go off duty. I told her exactly who I was and asked her to let us take a shot of the patient as he slept. She agreed, provided we disinfected our camera equipment and wore protective gowns and masks. We did this and were standing just inside the doorway of his special cubicle with the camera running when, suddenly, his eyes opened and he looked straight at me. Realising that there were going to be repercussions, I told him, for the record, that I was from the BBC and that his wife had signed a contract with ITN for his exclusive interview. He probably wasn't in a fit state to appreciate the significance of what I had just told him. He smiled and told us how happy he was to be alive. He chattered on about the miracle of it all until he fell asleep again. It was wonderful to see him recover like that as it dawned on him that he was back in the land of the living, with another chance. We thanked the nurse for all her help. She went off duty and we quietly left the hospital. Back at base Desmond Taylor was delighted and gave the cameraman a bonus.

Neither the hospital management nor the ITN reporter, when he returned from lunch, knew anything about our chat with Mr West, until the BBC TV News led their 6 o'clock programme with the story. Then the phones to Desmond Taylor went wild. His delight at getting a scoop turned to anger as he rushed from his office to tell me he was being threatened with a writ for infringing ITN's copyright. The hospital was furious because I hadn't bothered to ask their permission. I told him that ITN should have protected their interests more efficiently. In truth I couldn't have cared less what they threatened but I accepted responsibility for the way we had got the story. To my surprise the editor finally capitulated to pressure from the opposition and gave ITN our interview for their ten o'clock news bulletin.

Mr West eventually came round but only lasted forty-six days. He died from a 'suddenly overwhelming infection.' The first completely successful heart transplant didn't come until 1979 at Papworth Hospital, Cambridge, when the patient, Keith Castle, went on to survive for five years.

CHAPTER 12

MARDI IN DISTRESS

One night my sister, Mardi, phoned me from her home in Bremerhaven sounding extremely upset. She told me what a terrible time she was having with her husband, Klaus: it was the first inkling I'd had of any trouble between them. She seemed desperate to escape with their young child, Claudia, but Klaus had taken away her passport. Between the sobs, I got the impression that he was physically ill-treating my sister... that was enough for me.

I discussed the situation with my father and we agreed that I should catch the overnight ferry from Harwich to Bremerhaven, but would not tell Mardi I was coming. We didn't want to alert Klaus and put him on his guard. The plan was to extricate my sister and her daughter with as little drama as possible and bring them back to England.

It turned out that their marriage had not been good almost from the start. She had met Klaus, a car mechanic, when she was working as a hairdresser aboard a cruise ship. She had later joined him in Australia on a £10 assisted passage that was on offer. They married in Adelaide where Claudia was born. Klaus was just looking for an easy way of life and wasn't interested in getting a proper job, drinking a lot and womanising. Mardi stuck it for three years before returning to England with their daughter. Klaus soon followed but didn't want to stay in England, even though there was the promise of a good job and somewhere to live in Brighton, near our parents. Two days after he arrived they were on their way back to Bremerhaven, but the marriage problems just grew worse.

When the ferry docked in Bremerhaven, at about 8.30 the next morning, I phoned Mardi from the quayside. She sobbed and said how terrible it was that I was so far away. I said 'I'm not. I'm here and about to get a taxi to your house.'

When I knocked on her door I could see the relief on her face, but there was also fear. What was Klaus' reaction going to be? Fortunately he was out and we had time to catch up. We also made an appointment to see a local woman lawyer to try to force him to give Mardi her passport. I had already booked a berth for Mardi and Claudia on the return ferry to England later in the week.

When Klaus came home Mardi looked really worried and hid in the kitchen: I felt even more angry that he could make her feel so scared. He was clearly taken by surprise. I was the last person he'd expected to see. When I told him we weren't happy with the way he was treating Mardi and that I was here to take her and the child back to England, I think he was momentarily lost for words. I'd expected him to lose his temper but he was on the defensive and after a while he left the house.

The next few days were awful, especially for Mardi. Klaus had told his friends and relatives what was happening and I remember a few shouts of abuse, but Mardi was taking heart and began packing. A day or two later when we went to see the lawyer, Klaus was asked to join us ... and reluctantly he did. The lawyer left him in no doubt that he had no legal right to stop Mardi going to England with her daughter.

My mother Lucy,
and my sister Margaret.

It was an anxious time. As we were walking up the gangplank to board the ferry home Klaus turned up, maybe in a last effort to get Mardi to change her mind, but there was no turning back. We were soon at sea. From Harwich, Mardi and Claudia returned to Brighton to stay with our parents.

Once her divorce was finalised, Mardi took a job with American Express. When it was realised that she could speak German she was offered a good position at their office in where of all places? Bremerhaven. She took it. Later on she met and married Volker, a wealthy industrialist in the Bremerhaven shipping business. They had a daughter Christine and all went well for years, until one Boxing Day, when he hadn't turned up

84

for lunch, Mardi drove to his office to see if he was there and he was ... caught in the act with a Vietnamese stripper. Until then she had never suspected any infidelity.

When Mardi phoned me she was at a loss for words. She couldn't really understand what had gone wrong. This time I flew to Germany. Volker was in the garden waiting for me to arrive. Mardi peered through the kitchen window as we talked but what can be said in these situations? Volker was not an aggressive man. I liked him, so I asked him if this dalliance with the stripper was just a one-off aberration. He didn't seem too sure. Was it something he could quickly get out of his system? He thought for a few seconds and then said it might take him a year. I thought to myself that this guy must be joking ... maybe he's just kinky.

Volker wouldn't be drawn into any detail, only that he fancied Vietnamese ladies. But whatever happened, he said, he would look after Mardi and money would not be a problem. Mardi and I did a tour of the red light district of Bremerhaven in the daft hope of finding the Vietnamese lady in question, but there were just so many of them, parading around the street in various stages of undress and all looking pretty much alike. For all we knew, there could easily be more than just one Vietnamese lady in Volker's life. Finally, we gave up and went home.

Mardi and Volker are still married but live apart, Mardi in a lovely apartment in town and Volker in his large house in a park, with little signs of the Orient dotted around him. Now, at seventy-eight, he is not a healthy man and he is lucky that Mardi is prepared to spend so much of her time doing her bit to look after him.

CHAPTER 13

A JUNGLE MURDER HUNT

Self-styled Black Power leader, Michael X, became the first non-white person in Britain to be charged with incitement to violence under the new Race Relations Act. The press had glamorised his reputation in the late nineteen sixties and early seventies as someone who might improve opportunities for young black people in the face of discrimination. Michael X, real name Michael de Freitas, aka Abdul Malik, was a hustler. He had borrowed the X from Malcolm X, the American black power activist and set about making a name for himself in Notting Hill as the voice of reason, on behalf of underprivileged black youth. His own background in Britain had been that of rent collector and enforcer for the notorious slum landlord racketeer Peter Rachman, also in Notting Hill.

Michael X was also a drug dealer and brothel keeper, but he had established the Black House in Islington as a cultural centre for young blacks, with the backing of a young millionaire, Nigel Samuel, one of numerous wealthy white Liberals who were his benefactors and often his 'customers' for dope. In an interview I got with Michael at the Black House, he attempted to justify his criminal activity and violence on the streets as the only way to make the white establishment listen.

My bosses at the BBC timidly decided not to broadcast the interview for legal reasons; they were nervous and unsure of the workings of the new race law. So I locked the interview away in a drawer, figuring that one day it might come in useful. In the meantime Michael was awaiting trial at the Old Bailey charged with 'extortion and demanding money with menaces.' He decided to skip bail and flee back to his native Trinidad in the West Indies, rather than go to all the trouble and expense of extradition. Scotland Yard and the Home Office reckoned they were better off without him and did nothing. He was now Trinidad's problem.

One day an agency story from Trinidad came into my office, based on the finding of a man's body hidden in the garden of a house in Christina Gardens, Arima, about half-an-hour's drive from the capital, Port-of-Spain. The house was rented by Michael de Freitas, Michael X, and the police were looking for him. When Michael returned to Trinidad he had formed a gang which he ostentatiously named the Black Liberation Army, which attracted a lot of local publicity and created unease in government circles. Trinidad was still recovering from a mutiny in its army and the last thing wanted was someone else stirring up political trouble in the name of Black Power. Anyway, I persuaded the Editor that this story was probably the start of something much bigger and he should let me fly out there with a TV news crew to investigate. He agreed.

Gordon Carr, the BBC producer who investigated the Michael X story with me in the UK, Trinidad and in the jungle in Guyana.

While we were en route another body had been found in Michael X's garden, this time it was of a woman, Gale Benson, the daughter of an English Conservative Member of Parliament, Leonard Plugge. Michael X, who had been giving a lecture in Georgetown, Guyana when the bodies were uncovered, was now on the run, believed to be heading for Brazil. On arrival at Piarco airport, Trinidad, we caught up with the news and flew the short hop across the Gulf of Paria to Georgetown, Guyana. With my producer, Gordon Carr, I set about tracing some of Michael's contacts amongst his old friends from Notting Hill.

One of them was a barber, who had given Michael a very short haircut and shaved off his beard. The news that the police were looking for him was, by now, all over the local radio. The barber told us that a clean-shaven Michael was now heading south, hoping to find a route through the jungle to Brazil, by river. We hired an old Land Rover, bought a map and with a few provisions and bottled water to last a couple of days, set out from Georgetown towards the town of Buxton on Guyana's Atlantic coast.

We were eventually directed to the Rockstone trail, an old

Amerindian route to the Essequibo River, the gateway to the vast interior, which eventually merges into Brazil. It is a favourite area among intrepid big game hunters, but even for them it is difficult and dangerous terrain. Clearly, Michael was never going to get anywhere near his goal. The trail is narrow, about six feet wide, through very thick equatorial jungle plagued by mosquitoes and full of deadly snakes and other exotic wildlife, including sleek black leopards. It was getting dark by the time Michael reached the trail and there was hardly any moonlight piercing the giant trees on either side. He was neither armed, nor prepared with food or water for a journey that might have taken him many days. Even if he had reached the mighty Essequibo, he would have needed the help of the none too friendly river tribes and a canoe to make further progress.

Georgetown had mobilised its police force, which was soon closing in on him. He was exhausted, his sandals broken apart, when he came upon an Amerindian bushman's rickety bamboo shack. The man, Victor Bishop, was frightened when he saw the stranger enter his camp and grabbed his cutlass. Michael told him not to be scared, he just wanted somewhere to rest for the night. In the morning he would move off towards the river. 'My enemies are after me. Black people in my own country have let me down.'

It took several hours for Trinidadian detectives, who had flown to Georgetown, to reach the jungle. There were fourteen of them, heavily armed and just after midnight they fanned out around the camp. As dawn broke and a thin light exposed Bishop's shack, where both men were sleeping, they pounced. The first Michael knew of the police's arrival was when a heavy hand grabbed his collar and a revolver was pointed at his forehead.

'There's no need for that,' Michael said, 'I'll come quietly.'

By the time we arrived Michael had already been arrested. Under heavy guard he was driven back to Georgetown and put on a plane to Trinidad. When I spoke to Mr Bishop about his encounter with Michael X, he was still so scared and upset about the intrusion into his forest world, that the end of a smouldering cigarette he kept in his mouth was burning his lips, but he just left it there.

The discovery of the bodies at Michael's home, Christina

Gardens, Arima, was being given front page treatment both in Trinidad and Guyana as the most sensational killings since the murders of Boysie Singh. Singh was an Indian gangster who, in the nineteen forties, murdered countless immigrants bound for Port-of-Spain. Having paid their fares they were robbed of the rest of their wealth at sea and thrown to the sharks.

From the moment police brought Michael to headquarters, in Port-of-Spain, they were unable to penetrate his defence, which remained throughout sixteen hours of questioning, quite simple: that he knew absolutely nothing about the murders and that it was a political frame-up by members of his former gang or the police. What kind of person did they think he was, returning to Trinidad to do his best for people and then arranging to kill his own countrymen?

By renting a ranch-style bungalow set in a lush quarter-acre of garden in a middle-class area of Arima, Michael tried to give himself an air of respectability. With him in the house were two of his most trusted friends from his Black House days in London, Stanley Abbott and Steve 'Innocent' Yeates, both Trinidadians. During the first month of his stay there was a steady stream of petty criminals from the poorer districts of Port-of-Spain who had known Michael, Abbott, or Yeates in their schooldays, or in England. He enjoyed playing the role of prodigal son returned from Europe with influence and wealth, the man-about-town. He also invited a few politicians who he thought might one day form a strong opposition to the government of Prime Minister Eric Williams, who had guided Trinidad into Independence. Michael brought his wife Desiree from England and their two daughters, who loved entertaining their guests in a style that they never known back in Islington. There was a maid, in white cap and pinafore, serving tea at the sound of a bell, in the style of the old colonial slave masters whom Michael professed to detest. His biggest social coup was a visit from John Lennon and Yoko Ono, which of course made headlines in the local newspapers. He was also pictured as a friend of Muhammed Ali when the heavyweight champion came to Trinidad for a series of exhibition matches.

Michael, with his grand plans for Trinidad, fooled many people, but there were intelligent journalists in Port-of-Spain who could see through him. His so-called Black Liberation Army was a joke, but not to the police who were keeping an eye on him from a distance: a number of raids on police stations for arms and ammunition were being blamed on him. There was also growing police concern about members of his gang dealing in drugs. The influence Michael had over his gang owed much to his belief in the dark power, that when he was possessed by the spirit Ogun, one of the ancient Gods of the Yoruba tribe, he was indestructible. It helped Michael to be either charismatic or menacing, as and when it suited him. While he was in jail awaiting trial I once got a phone call from a prison officer, who was influenced by Michael, with a message to go to visit him.

Life at Christina Gardens started to go wrong for Michael and his gang with the arrival of Gale Benson, accompanied by her boyfriend Hakim Jamal, a rather impressionable young man from Boston in America, who had converted to Islam after hearing a Malcolm X speech. But Hakim proved not to have the intellect or spiritual sincerity to be anything more than a scrounger, trying to cash in on feelings of guilt which some celebrities and white intelligentsia, on both sides of the Atlantic, expressed about the plight of black people.

Michael X (real name Michael de Freitas, aka Abdul Malik). He had his beard shaved off before trying to escape through the jungle in Guyana.

He had met Vanessa Redgrave in California. She had been impressed by his big ideas and had invited him to stay with her whenever he was in London. Naturally, he took her offer sincerely and so gained entrée to the smart Chelsea upper middle-class, including Gale Benson, who was educated at the French Lycée in London and fluent in French and Spanish. Her family were direct descendants of Sir John Hawkins, a seafaring slave-master from Plymouth and kinsman of Sir Francis Drake. What an opportunity for the likes of Hakim Jamal; no wonder he quickly ensnared her. Having converted to Islam himself he gave Gale a Muslim name… Hale Kimga…an anagram of Hakim and Gale.

She was in love with Hakim, but after some weeks as guests

of Michael in Christina Gardens, she became concerned that her boyfriend was so besotted with him. It was as though Hakim had become one of Michael's lap dogs and she needed to know more about the shady side of Michael X. On two occasions he caught her looking at private papers in his study when she thought he was out of sight. She was sharp enough to talk her way out of trouble or so she thought at the time. In fact, Michael had already decided that something would have to be done about her curiosity. Gale wasn't the only one on Michael's blacklist. One of the latest recruits to his Black Liberation Army, Joseph Skerritt, was a young man from Belmont in Port-of-Spain, who had been given work, initially, in the garden. But he became frightened at some of the schemes Michael was hatching to raise money, which involved kidnapping.

Gale became so worried about Michael's dangerous side that she wrote to her twin brother in England telling him that Hakim had completely fallen under Michael's control and was getting mixed up in ventures that could land them all in jail. Meanwhile, Michael was spreading the rumour among his men that Gale could be a spy working for MI5 through her English connections: or maybe the CIA. Sometimes Michael's imagination, fuelled by marijuana, was on the edge of psychosis, but nobody really guessed that Gale was in real danger. Hakim had contacts among the Boston underworld gang, The Black Panthers and had let it slip that he knew one of their assassins who went by the African name, Kidogo. Michael got the man's real name and address from Hakim, while he was under the influence of the weed and hired Kidogo to come to Trinidad for a 'special job.'

The name on Kidogo's passport, when he flew into Piarco airport, was Marvin Deane. Now there was this short, stocky, bull-necked man strutting about Christina Gardens in African robes but rarely talking to anyone. Michael had also told him not to take any notice of what his friend Hakim might say. One morning Kidogo went into Port-of-Spain to buy a cutlass of the weight and length he liked and back in Christina Gardens he filed it into the shape of a spear. Some of the men learned what Michael was intending to do, which they found difficult to comprehend; they asked why Gale couldn't be put on a plane back to England, but Michael said he wanted blood and gave the order for them to start digging a hole which was not to be visible from the house. There were pleas to spare the woman but no-one dared to disobey. Gale, who had risen early while her boyfriend slept, was brought to the hole by Stanley Abbott who jumped into it with her. Kidogo followed and started slashing at her with his cutlass. Gale fought bravely, with her flailing arms trying to ward off the blows and was being badly cut about the body. For a hired assassin Kidogo was doing an incompetent job and Steve Yeates, standing by the edge of the hole, could stand it no longer. He jumped in, grabbed the cutlass from Kidogo, raised it vertically with the point against her throat and plunged it deep. With a moan she fell back, but her feet were still moving when the men started to shovel earth over her. When the grave was levelled they planted lettuce. Michael's wife and family, Hakim and two other guests had no idea where Gale had gone. Michael's men were threatened that if they breathed a word the same thing would happen to them and their families. Kidogo left for America.

Young Skerritt, who knew nothing of the murder, could see that the men were under a lot of strain, particularly Hakim who couldn't understand why Gale had suddenly vanished along with all her possessions. He was suspicious but he too was scared to ask many questions. Skerritt became increasingly worried about the sorts of activity the gang were planning. They were going to involve him in the robbery of a police station to steal uniforms which would be used later in the kidnapping of a bank manager. Skerritt refused to take part. Michael told him instead he was to dig a soakaway pit in the garden which was also for refuse. Skerritt obliged, happy to be just a gardener. Michael's right-hand man, Stanley Abbott, helped dig the hole beneath a large sapodilla tree. When they'd finished he grabbed Skerritt and jumped into the hole with him, handing him to Michael who was brandishing the cutlass used to kill Gale Benson. He drew the razor-sharp blade across Skerritt's neck, completely severing the jugular artery. Skerritt screamed out: 'Oh God! Ah go tell! Ah go tell.' With that, Michael seized a large stone and smashed it down on his victim's head. He lay silent. They filled in the grave and again planted lettuce. In the anxious days that followed a dejected Hakim returned to America. Steve Yeates, who had finally put Gale Benson out of her torment, was drowned in a suspicious swimming accident off the north coast.

One weekend, when Michael accepted an offer to give a

lecture in Georgetown, a mysterious fire totally destroyed the house at Christina Gardens. The police discovered the graves. The lettuce beds the men had planted had sunk in the rain because the criminals had forgotten to pack the earth down properly. The hunt for Michael X began. From the time he was captured in Guyana and brought back to Trinidad the case made sensational local headlines. On the day that Michael first appeared in court at committal proceedings in 1972, hundreds of police were on duty to prevent barriers from being swept aside by people striving to catch a glimpse of him. In the little wooden court house there was standing room only.

There was so much noise that by the end of the hearing none of us journalists were sure exactly what legal points had been established. Neither were the lawyers, so the case was adjourned. That happened several times. When I visited Michael in the old Royal Gaol in Port-of-Spain he was having difficulty getting anyone from Trinidad to represent him. He had hoped that a barrister he knew in London, Lord Gifford, would fly out. However, Kenneth Foster, a barrister from the nearby Caribbean island of St. Lucia, quickly volunteered his services. He had a successful reputation in murder cases. Michael told him that money would be no object; 'John Lennon and Yoko, my best friends in America, will see to that.'

It was pretty clear to me that it was going to be a long time before the case against Michael ever came to trial. There were so many hindrances. Foster was having difficulty getting another qualified lawyer into Trinidad to help him and complained to the Court that the Trinidad Immigration Authority was deliberately procrastinating, which was true. Foster argued that he was entitled to the same advantages as the Crown prosecutors who had no shortage of legal assistance. Michael in his cool blue and white striped prison suit seemed to be basking in his notoriety and enjoyed waving to his public whenever he could. He told the Court several times that for them to press ahead, when de did not have proper legal representation, would be a miscarriage of justice and he was right. So Foster was given time to prepare his case, which was no easy task considering he knew little about Michael X, his background or the case against him, beyond the headlines. Michael told him that if he wanted someone to brief him on his history, he should contact me as I was the only English correspondent in Trinidad, at that time, who knew much about his background. Foster duly made contact.

The BBC in London was receiving short news stories from me every day, but as the headlines grew, they decided that the saga merited a special news documentary and that no matter how long the case dragged on I should stay in Trinidad to piece it all together into a blockbuster of a detective story.

In those days money seemed to be no object. I was given a suite at the Trinidad Hilton Hotel, which had a large balcony with wonderful tropical plants, overlooking the Queen's Park Savannah, close to the town centre. Georgina Masson, the ebullient head of the Hilton's public relations, made sure that I had everything I needed, even replacing the vibrant flowers and drinks in my suite each day. Word about my lifestyle at the Hilton made diary stories for the local papers. I had no shortage of people volunteering information about Michael X, some useful, some a waste of time. Everyone, it seemed, wanted to get in on story, enabling me to build up an extraordinary list of contacts.

It was a particularly wise move to engage two trustworthy taxi drivers, with cars large enough to take all our television kit and which were in good roadworthy condition. Exclusive use of their Cadillacs at any time of the day or night, seven days a week, cost £50 a day each which was a lot of money then, about £500 apiece in today's money, but well worth it. The drivers knew the Port-of-Spain crime scene and were familiar with the world of Obeah, or Shango, as they call it in Trinidad, which is really embraced by the fascinating traditional West African religion of Orisha. I was introduced to some of their leaders and welcomed into their chapels, meeting places or shrines.

As time went on the bills at the Hilton were mounting alarmingly, but the BBC were pleased with the way the story was going and told me to put the hotel in touch with the Corporation's accounts manager in London who would settle all bills: not something they would do these days, for sure. I had a spare weekend and asked some of my Trinidad friends in newspapers to help me hire a schooner with plenty of deck space for dancing and live music. There would be food and drink and they were to invite a small, interesting group of people whose connections might be valuable in my Michael X investigation. It all went brilliantly, as we sailed around the

94

islands off Trinidad under a bright, tropical moon, a light breeze billowing the sails.

Trinidadians do not need any encouragement when it comes to enjoying a party, especially if there's good food and drink. They are colourful, vibrant, brim-full of humour. Calypso and soca music are in their DNA: they know how to dance, as anyone who has ever experienced the Trinidad Carnival will tell you. It's not like watching white people dance...most of them moving round the floor as though they were shifting furniture, or jumping up and down, out of time with the music, just for exercise. With Caribbean people rhythm is in the soul. Anyway, my newspaper friends had chosen their guest list well, with a happy mixture of men and women who had a finger on the pulse of life in Trinidad.

It turned out to be a very important evening for me and not just for the useful contacts it produced. I met a very attractive, twenty-four-year old brunette, Rowena Scott, who had mesmer-

Rowena Scott as she was in 1972 when I first met her at the Trinidad Yacht Club while I was covering the Michael X story.

ising blue-green eyes. We felt a mutual attraction as we stood chatting on the jetty at Trinidad Yacht Club, before boarding the boat. Years later she was to become my wife, following the breakdown of my marriage to Gerry.

Through Rowena and her family many doors were opened and I became good friends with the pathologist in the Michael X case, Michael 'Mick' Healy and the Prime Minister's press advisor, George John. Rowena, at that time, was in Trinidad on holiday from Colombia where she was teaching English.

Unfortunately, a day or so after our cruise, I got a call from TV News in London to take a break from the Michael X investigation and to fly immediately to Panama. An English family, the Robertsons, had been attacked in their boat by a school of killer whales and had been drifting in the middle of the Pacific Ocean for thirty-seven days, crammed into a nine-foot dinghy. A Japanese fishing boat had picked them up and would be bringing them into Panama around dawn.

I was the nearest correspondent and arrived on the dockside in Panama in plenty of time to see the family being lifted ashore, hardly able to stand, their faces and hands covered in salt-water sores. They told me their amazing story of survival against the odds. The attack on their yacht had happened so swiftly they only had time to grab a few biscuits, oranges and lemons, a bag of onions and a tin of glucose sweets and one bottle of water between the five of them: mother, father and three children. The whales repeatedly battered the sailing boat with such ferocity that it sank within minutes. The family jumped onto some of the wooden debris, using it as a raft but it was leaking badly. Luckily they had managed to retrieve the dinghy, along with the meagre supplies. Once that was afloat, it was their only protection against the elements, heaving and pitching in the vastness of the Pacific. Their only fluids, when the water ran out, was rainwater and the blood of turtles they managed to catch as they came alongside. They had real luck to be spotted by Japanese fisherman, who were more than surprised to see anyone alive crouched in the bottom of that dinghy.

By 8am, I had wrapped up the story and needed to get it back to London as quickly as possible. There was an overnight flight from Panama which would mean the film could be broadcast the following day. The sound-recordist in my crew seemed to be very friendly with the opposition team who had arrived from ITN. He told me that they would be shipping their story on the same overnight flight and he would like to do the same. Without realising it he had handed me a golden opportunity to scoop the opposition.

I put together a package of film for him to take to the airport at the same time as ITN and ship it. What he did not know was that the film I had given him was unused, blank. While he was away I had arranged for a BBC producer to fly down from our office in New York to studios in Miami. I would send the real footage of the Robertson's rescue to her and by satellite she would then transmit it straight to London. It would be on the air that night.

When the sound recordist returned from shipping the dummy film, with an ETA the following day, I told him what was now going to happen. He was to take the real film to Miami on the next plane, on which he was already booked, where would be met at the airport by a lady producer from the BBC. He was to hand the package to her and then fly straight back to us in Panama. I didn't want to run the risk that he might talk to ITN. I wanted our film to get to Miami quickly and safely. It worked like a dream, though the sound-recordist was not best pleased to have been tricked into scooping his friends from ITN, nor to learn that they had been beaten by a whole day. But that's the way it goes sometimes.

CHAPTER 14

A RISKY MOVE

Back in Trinidad the long-awaited trial of Michael X was about to start at the Red House, an imposing beaux-arts structure originally built in 1897 to commemorate Queen Victoria's Diamond Jubilee, which is both the seat of Trinidad's parliament and of the assize court. It had been decided that Michael would be tried separately from the other men accused of being involved in the two murders at Christina Gardens and that there would only be one charge: the murder of Joseph Skerritt, who really had dug his own grave.

Hundreds of people crowded round the entrance to the Red House long before the court opened, resembling the start of a Trinidad-style fete at carnival time. The street vendors were out in force with their 'doubles', based on curried chickpeas, hand-held greasy delights popular as breakfast with people on their way to work, or curried beef goat and chicken roti, with the smell of hot pepper sauce and plenty of noise with blasting soca music from portable radios. Michael smiled at the enormous crowd as he was walked, handcuffed, into court.

Inside, it was a different picture, very much like the Old Bailey, except that the interior of courtroom number one was ringed by tall policemen, pin-smart in their white uniforms and caps, belt-brasses gleaming. As in England, the lawyers were lined up ready to do battle in their wigs and gowns. The public gallery was jammed with black ladies showing off their best cotton dresses and wide straw hats. A white hen, which had somehow found its way into court through a sea of legs, suddenly scuttled across the floor, cackling as it hopped out through an open window. A middle-aged women nearest to it gasped and backed away. 'Oh Gawd. Dat is a bad, bad sign. De Obeah man does come.' As Mr Justice Evan Rees solemnly entered the court the hubbub died down.

I decided to take a chance and openly film the proceedings from the outset, gambling that the policemen standing to attention around the court would assume that I must have been given special permission and wouldn't move a muscle to stop us. The cameraman and I just stepped out of the packed press benches and started filming, trying to give the impression that it was perfectly acceptable practice for an English TV crew.

Local reporters, watching, were taken aback but no-one protested, not even the pompous Attorney-General, Karl Hudson-Phillips who was prosecuting. We reckoned that we would need the afternoon session to complete our courtroom filming, so in the lunch break I went to the judge's chambers. He was sitting there, wigless, when I knocked and went in. I apologised for the intrusion and for having taken the liberty of filming in his court that morning; I had just assumed that it would be alright in Trinidad, considering the publicity the case was attracting.

The judge peered over his bi-focals. 'Would you be allowed to film in the Old Bailey?'

'Certainly not while the court was in session, your Honour,' I replied. 'they are not that progressive.'

He countered without hesitation, 'Well, I regard myself as a progressive judge and I give you permission to carry on filming.'

During the course of the afternoon, as the Attorney-General droned on with his outline of Skerritt's gruesome murder, I could see that he was increasingly irritated by the presence of the camera. He suddenly stopped talking and complained to the judge. 'I really must object to these people taking my picture', he said with his best, upper-class, English accent.

Judge Evan Rees stared at him. 'I have given them permission to film in my court,' he said. 'If you don't like it I suggest that's a matter you could take up with the cameraman. Maybe he doesn't really want to take your picture.'

The public gallery erupted into laughter, clearly pleased to see the Attorney-General being taken down a peg. He had dominated the early stage of the trial with an overbearing sense of his own importance. In the minds of a lot of ordinary Trinidadians, here was a black man with an Englishman inside him struggling to get out. Local reporters in the press gallery were amazed that a foreign TV team had got away with taking the only pictures of Michael X on trial for his life and wrote about us in their papers. The white-suited policemen guarding the courtroom interior looked relieved that the judge, most importantly, was happy. So were we.

At the end of six weeks of blood-curdling evidence Michael X was sentenced to be hanged for the murder of Joseph Skerritt. Two other men, Abbott and Chadee, were subsequently sentenced to death at a separate hearing into the Gale Benson murder.

Michael X remained in the condemned cell for two years and eight months while appeals were made on his behalf. He was not an easy prisoner and threatened several impressionable prison officers with Obeah, witchcraft spells. They provided him with a comfortable bed and supplies of marijuana and cigarettes to keep him calm.

His case was finally heard by the Judicial Committee of the Privy Council in London which serves as the supreme court for Trinidad's legal system. Sir Dingle Foot QC, who had a long record of fighting black people's causes both in Britain and in her colonies, fought Michael's case on the grounds of miscarriage of justice in the trial proceedings, but his argument was thrown out. There were other unsuccessful legal attempts to help Michael by Louis Blom-Cooper QC, who was the chairman of the influential Howard League for Penal Reform and by Geoffrey Robertson QC, the civil liberties lawyer.

On 16th May 1975, Michael X was finally led to the gallows in Port-of-Spain goal and hanged. The death penalty still exists in Trinidad.

CHAPTER 15

STORM CLOUDS OVER CYPRUS

For most of my working life as a journalist the Middle East was at war with itself. I had to have two passports, an extra for Israel. It saved a lot of problems at airports, trying to explain all the to-ing and fro-ing between trouble spots to suspicious immigration officials. If I was in Tel-Aviv and wanted to get to Beirut, I would stopover in Cyprus at the Ledra Palace Hotel to switch passports and have all my clothes cleaned in their excellent laundry. The Ledra Palace was a favourite among journalists because it stood, conveniently, on the Green Line dividing the Turkish and Greek communities.

The political landscape in Cyprus had been in turmoil since the British decolonised the island and Archbishop Makarios took over as its first President in 1960. The British had been reluctant to relinquish Cyprus because it had become their headquarters for the Middle East. There had been fierce fighting in the battle for self-government, led by the main independence movement, EOKA. In 1964, the United Nations established a peace-keeping force, but it failed to stop the political in-fighting between the Turkish community, mostly in the north of the island and the Greek Cypriots.

Archbishop Makarios, the so-called Father of the Nation, was so ruthless in trying to strengthen his control over the running of the country that other ambitious politicians, who had been his supporters through hard times, turned against him. There were four attempts at his assassination. During this period, in March 1970, I had flown in from Beirut to investigate the death threats.

One suspect was Polycarpos Georghiades, who had been Makarios' right-hand man for eight years and before that a leader in the EOKA struggle for independence. I tracked him down to the house of a friend and he agreed to do an interview, during which he vehemently denied any involvement in attempts to kill Makarios. He said people had mistakenly suspected him because some of the men who had already been detained in custody happened to be good friends of his. He sounded convincing enough to me, but I didn't know enough about his character to make a reliable judgement, but there were obviously others who could: five days after my interview with him he was abducted from Nicosia and murdered. His body was found by the side of a country road four miles outside the capital. He had been shot four times in the chest.

Rumours were rife of an imminent attempt to overthrow the Makarios government, some of them wrongly planting blame among the Turkish community. There was another attempt to kill the Archbishop, as he left the Presidential Palace by helicopter. Machine gun fire, coming from the roof of a high school, riddled the side of the helicopter, missing the Archbishop by inches. The pilot managed to guide the chopper over the palace building and land on a vacant lot on the other side, from where Makarios was rushed to safety. He was unharmed, but he wasn't seen in public for a few days and rumours started that maybe he had been hit and those around him were trying to keep it secret. I had a useful contact in the palace and was trying to persuade him to get me an exclusive interview with Makarios. Through the med-ium of the BBC, the President could show that he was still very much alive and in control. He would only need to do one interview; the World Service would tell everyone else. It was a long shot: every reporter in Nicosia wanted an interview.

Archbishop Makarios, President of Cyprus, after an assassination attempt on his life in 1970. I later exclusively interviewed him in hiding.

Late one Friday evening at the end of March 1970, a call came from my contact. I was to enter the Palace by a side door and to come alone. I left the Ledra Palace, making sure that none of the other journalists staying there saw me. I took a circuitous route on foot to the palace and my contact let me in. Makarios was alone in his vast study, smoking heavily. The ashtray on his desk was almost full. Calmly he told me that just before the attack on his helicopter he had received secret papers outlining an imminent coup d'etat.

The danger, he said, was not coming from Turkish-Cypriot politicians, but from within, among an elite group, some in his own cabinet, who disagreed with his policies on the future of Cyprus.

Given the volatile nature of Cypriot politics, the taped interview was clearly important, but it was by now very late on a Friday, too late for any major news programmes. The Archbishop wanted to know what sort of prominence he might be given by the BBC. He asked if his interview could be sent to London, but held over the weekend until Monday. I told him that might be possible, but only if he could guarantee that he would not give interviews to anyone else. He agreed and so did my boss in London, but it made for a very anxious weekend, expecting that at any minute some other reporters would burst into the hotel boasting about their great interviews with Makarios. In the event everything went according to plan. On Monday the World Service did an excellent job with the exclusive interview, beaming it around the globe.

Over the next four years the storm clouds continued to gather over Cyprus. On the 15th July, 1974 The Greek National Guard mounted a coup against President Makarios and replaced him with Nikos Sampson a former EOKA (Union with Greece) fighter and assassin. It was a short-lived coup but it gave Ankara the pretext it needed to intervene to protect the Turkish minority on the island. Makarios, who had now gone into hiding, was secretly flown out of Cyprus by the RAF to London. He died of a heart attack in 1977.

The Turks complained that the Greek-Cypriot army's action was in contravention of a United Nations Treaty guaranteeing the safety of the Turkish-Cypriot community. The Americans, though they had their Sixth Fleet in the Mediterranean, were not moved to react except to say they were glad to see the back of President Makarios, because they believed his politics were too favourable to the Soviet Union and they didn't want to see him become another Castro. President Nixon, showed no further interest in Cyprus. He was far too bogged down by the Watergate scandal, which ended his Presidency. He reckoned that the British could easily protect their own interests. They held their military bases in Cyprus in perpetuity.

What happened next, as we news reporters who were Middle East watchers could have foretold, would have been a comedy of errors if it had not been so calamitous.

The British High Command understood the warning signs from Ankara and organised reinforcements to the Sovereign Base Areas of Cyprus, which included sending more than three thousand extra soldiers, four Puma helicopters, two squadrons of Scorpion light tanks of the 16th/5th Lancers and the Royal Horse Guards and twelve RAF Phantoms. Offshore, on the carrier HMS Hermes, 41 Royal Marines Commando stood readied for action, but their services were never called upon.

The British could probably have prevented a Turkish invasion, or at least have offered some deterrent, by ordering the Royal Navy to block the narrow waterway between the northern Coast of Cyprus and the Turkish mainland. In Cyprus two infantry battalions with supporting weaponry were stood down. The Royal Marines remained offshore and the British Army on the island, in the event of a Turkish attack, was ordered only to protect the military families living in the Sovereign bases at Larnaca and Limassol and not to enter confrontation with the Turks. Though the Greek-Cypriots pleaded with Britain to stop the conflict, the British Foreign Secretary at the time, James Callaghan, replied that in his view British military force would only exacerbate and complicate the situation. The Turkish army launched their attack, Operation Attila, by sea and by air-drop on the northern plain between Nicosia and the Kyrenia Mountains.

In anticipation of a Turkish strike, nobody knew exactly when it might be, two BBC and ITN news crews were travelling across the plain in separate cars, when the ITN vehicle had a puncture and stopped to change the tyre. The BBC reporter, Michael Sullivan, offered to help but was waived on to Kyrenia. Not long after, he was well out of sight the ITN team. With the help of their reporter, Mike Nicholson, the tyre was mended and they were about to restart the journey when the drone of Turkish planes was heard. Suddenly the sky was thick with Turkish paratroops. The ITN's camera was quickly in action capturing the drama as it unfolded around them. It was a brilliant scoop and they were lucky that none of the Turkish paras took a shot at them. From a distance the 'rifle mike' ITN was using to capture the sound, might easily have been mistaken for a hand-held rocket launcher.

ITN's good fortune held for the rest of the invasion. A Turkish officer who spoke good English was among the first to land and

Martin Bell, veteran war correspondent, who served part of his National Service with the Suffolk Regiment in Cyprus during EOKA's armed rebellion against the British; myself who interviewed President Makarios after an assassination attempt; and Michael Sullivan who narrowly missed out on the Turkish paratroop invasion of northern Cyprus.

grasping the chance for some extraordinary publicity, took the ITN crew along with this troops to film the fighting when the Turks encountered resistance from the Greek-Cypriot army.

All ITN's early footage was shipped back to London via Ankara and shown that night, giving ITN the edge on the rest of the world's press. It was spectacular footage, as I recall. There was nothing any of the BBC's numerous reporters, elsewhere on the island, could do to compete against that kind of luck. Michael Sullivan was left tearing his hair out along the coast in Kyrenia, while being blamed for the BBC's poor coverage by Alan Protheroe, his London editor, a colonel, no less in, the Territorial Army.

In a military situation, like Cyprus, one of the first objectives of the invading force would be to secure the airport or bomb the runways so that they could not be used to quickly bring in further reinforcements. That is what happened. The Greek Cypriot army put up fierce resistance but they were no match for the Turkish paras as they blasted their way towards Nicosia airport. At the time the airport was controlled jointly by the RAF and the British-led UN force.

On the morning of 21st July, 1974, as the Turks started fire-bombing the runways, the commander of the British UN contingent, Brigadier Francis Henn, recalled seeing an un-welcome development, as all male RAF personnel, led by their station commander, began abandoning the base to join a convoy being formed to take women and children into the capital. They were brought to the Hilton Hotel, Nicosia, to join all the other civilian refugees fleeing the Sovereign bases as part of a British evacuation programme. The Brigadier's UN British contingent, he complained, was neither consulted on nor even informed about the evacuation plan. He observed that the British government's policy, throughout the crisis of 1974, amounted to an obsession with just protecting its Sovereign Base Areas, while subordinating the interests of the UN and those of the Republic of Cyprus.

With little standing in their way, the Turkish army was able to secure thirty-seven per cent of the island before a ceasefire was called: nothing has changed to this day. Over four decades, I have watched the two community leaders, Raul Denktash for the Turks and Glafcos Clerides for the Greeks meeting regularly to find a solution to partition, but getting absolutely nowhere. They have made it a pointless job for life.

A tragic end to the 1974 crisis on Cyprus was the death of a young BBC sound-recordist, Ted Stoddart, who triggered a landmine. He was in a car leading a four-vehicle convoy of journalists and photographers to the northern coast via Lapithos. Turkish soldiers had mined a section of the road overnight. Ted's car stopped and he got out to warn those behind, stepping on a mine in the process. As he staggered about several other mines were triggered. Shrapnel flew in all directions. Four other journalists were injured, two seriously.

CHAPTER 16

DEATH ON THE NILE

The phone in my room at the Ledra Palace rang early, as the dry warmth of a Mediterranean morning was just making itself known on the balcony outside. It was the Foreign Desk at BBC News. Britain had freed the Palestinian bomber, Leila Khaled, from custody as part of an exchange deal for the lives of fifty-six American and European hostages who were being held aboard a hijacked plane at Dawson's Field, a remote desert airstrip near Zarga, Jordan, formerly an RAF base. The foreign editor said he believed she was heading for Beirut. Go find her.

Leila Khaled was a demure young woman who looked as though she would not harm a fly. She had shot to public attention as The Poster Girl of Palestinian Militancy when she and an accomplice posing as her husband, boarded El Al Flight 219 from Amsterdam to New York, somehow hiding firearms and hand grenades. But Israeli sky marshals overpowered her and shot the man. The pilot then diverted to Heathrow and Leila Khaled was held in custody at Ealing police station. This wasn't her first involvement in hi-jacking and her capture made the headlines. Despite that, her first visitor in the Ealing police cell was a young immigration officer, clasping a sheaf of forms to be filled in. His first question to her was: 'Why have you entered Britain without a valid visa?' The police guard could barely believe his ears. Leila Khaled's image by then, brandishing a Kalashnikov assault rifle, had joined that of Che Guevara in the media world.

The Palestinian freedom fighters had corralled four hijacked planes at Dawson's field and taken three hundred and ten hostages. They emptied three of the planes and blew them up. They then separated out all the Americans and Jews and freed the rest. Among these passengers were U.S. State Department officials and a rabbi. There were frantic calls between Washington and London. In exchange for the lives of the hostages the hijackers demanded the release of Leila Khaled with other Palestinians imprisoned on terrorist charges in Germany and Switzerland.

All this was humiliating for King Hussein of Jordan. The exploitation of Jordanian territory by militant Arab Palestinian activists posed a direct threat to his Hashemite monarchy. He declared martial law and on 16th September, 1970 deployed his forces, entering into the Palestinian controlled territory, nearly triggering a regional war involving Israel, Syria and Iraq. Fortunately the King's well-trained army was swiftly victorious and trans-Atlantic diplomacy struck a deal with the Palestine Liberation Front, the PLF, freeing all the hostages, including Leila Khaled in London.

Leila had been born in Haifa, a busy industrial port on Israel's northern coast. Her family had fled to Lebanon in 1948 as part of the Palestinian exodus which followed the creation of the Jewish state. I had a few contacts within the PLF in Beirut and after she had been freed in London I thought that she was probably with relatives, in Tyre or in Amman.

King Hussein was still trying to restore order in his Kingdom following the clashes with the Palestinian forces and the airport wasn't fully operational. I was attempting to get permission to fly in with the Red Cross and their medical supplies, but fate intervened. The phone in my Beirut hotel room rang. Again, it was the Foreign Desk: 'Stop what you're doing and go to Cairo. Nasser is dead.'

We didn't know at that stage how President Gamal Abdel Nasser had died; perhaps he had been assassinated. There had been attempts on his life before. I booked myself and the TV News crew onto the last plane into Cairo, arriving around midnight. Normally at that time the airport would be practically empty, but on this occasion it was seething with people in a state of high excitement. Outside the building, the road into the city was choked with cars, carts, buses and taxis honking their way into the centre. In the early hours there must have been over a million people surrounding the 12th century Al Asr Mosque. It became clear that the President had died of a heart attack.

He was regarded by many of his countrymen as the Father of Reform, who, after nationalising the Suez Canal, had introduced a series of socialist changes to transform Egypt's economy. Now, it seemed, the nation was in tears.

On the morning of his funeral there were an estimated five million mourners jamming the centre. The weight of their numbers was pushing down fully grown palm trees. My

108

cameraman, Bob Poole, the sound recordist and I linked arms into a triangle to stabilise ourselves in the hysterical crowd. A small boy nearby was about to be trampled underfoot, so we grabbed him, pushing him into our protective triangle. There were screaming people falling off tall billboards into the Nile, the surging crowd growing more and more out of control. We managed to press our way to the edge of the crowd to a block of flats with a balcony on the first floor. Bob hammered on the door and thrust a fistful of notes into the owner's hand: he let us film from the vantage point of his apartment, from where we had a magnificent view of the throng stretching as far as the eye could see, filling every inch of space.

A gun carriage, bearing Nasser's coffin, protected by columns of soldiers, came slowly across the Nile bridge. The crowd surged towards them and suddenly we saw the entire bridge rolling up and down as though it might collapse at any moment. The formal funeral procession and all the government ministers following it were stopped in their tracks. The coffin was grabbed from the gun carriage and carried away by the crowd. We watched it bobbing up and down atop a sea of arms and heads, until it disappeared from sight. Everyone wanted to touch that coffin.

Although President Nasser had his detractors who didn't like his authoritarian pattern of military dictatorial rule, he was an iconic figure in the Arab world: a hero to the weeping mourners and to many others. By morning his coffin had been returned by the people, intact, to the Al Asr Mosque. Later Nasser lay in state at the Presidential palace. His successor was Anwar Sadat who promised further social change, but the spread of radical Islamist ideology was taking hold in Egypt and Henry Kissinger, then U.S. Secretary of State, forecast that Sadat would not last very long. He was right. Sadat served as Egypt's president from October 1977 until he was shot dead in 1981. Fundamentalist army officers ordered his assassination, which took place during a military parade being held to commemorate Yom Kipper in Israel.

CHAPTER 17

HARD KNOCKS IN NABLUS

It was time to head for Cyprus again, pick up my fresh laundry and passports, then head for Tel-Aviv. There were disturbing stories that the Israeli army was overstepping the mark in their treatment of Palestinian civilians: this time clubbing school children suspected of throwing stones at their armoured patrol vehicles. Israeli soldiers were said to have charged into classrooms beating up any youngsters they thought were troublemakers.

Early one morning, long before the children got there, we had installed ourselves inside a school in Gaza, with the headmaster's permission. We were just waiting to see what happened. The Israeli soldiers in that area knew exactly when the pupils would start arriving each day and they knew full well that a few stones would be hurled at them, which simply bounced off their armour-plating. They could easily have held up their patrol until later, when the kids were safely inside the school, but they wanted a bit of action ... anything to provoke a Palestinian reaction.

Inevitably, a few stones were hurled at them. Instead of driving on, two army vehicles stopped and half a dozen soldiers, led by a young officer, charged into the school clubbing some of the teenagers while shoving the protesting teachers out of the way. They didn't realise they were being filmed and carried on for several minutes beating children, leaving some of them bleeding on the ground. When the officer finally saw our camera whirring away he rushed over and demanded we give him the film. We refused. He threatened to arrest us and confiscate the camera. We told him we could not let him take it, but we would go with him to speak with a senior officer. Whatever happened the events of that morning would be broadcast one way or another. The officer was unsure how to deal with the situation but took us to his group headquarters. There an older officer, a major, was more decisive. He took the film from the camera and told us to get lost, hinting that we should think ourselves lucky. We tried to get the film returned through official channels in Tel-Aviv and even though I did broadcast a piece about the brutality at the school on BBC radio news, we never saw the film again.

It was not unusual for the Israeli army to launch itself into some action or other, regardless of who might be filming or just observing, as the soldiers considered themselves to be a law unto themselves.

We were filming a peaceful Palestinian march in the ancient city of Nablus, thirty miles to the North of Jerusalem in the highlands of the River Jordan's west bank. Although it has been in occupied Israeli territory since the 1967 Six Day War, it was governed by the Palestine National Authority. The marchers, several thousand strong, never intended to go beyond the walls of the old city. We were filming from the rear of the crowd when suddenly Israeli soldiers entered the city and started firing into the air, causing a panic. The crowd turned, fleeing in all directions, but there was no easy escape route. Old Nablus is a rabbit-warren of narrow alleyways and we were caught up in the chaos. I fell on a pile of bricks, damaging my lower spine as people trampled over me.

It was not the first time I had injured my back on an assignment. In Lagos, I was going to see some officials on the twentieth floor of the new Independence building. At the third floor the lift failed, shuddered and then, full of people, plummeted down. In a matter of seconds it had careered to the bottom falling onto a giant spring, which sent it hurtling up and down until it finally came to rest about a foot below the ground floor. I felt as though my legs were being driven up through my body as I crouched in a corner of the lift. There was a dreadful scramble to get through the gap to the ground floor. I lay there waiting until it was empty, when a couple of attendants helped me out. It took me days to recover from the shock. Thank God the lift hadn't failed on the top floor. I had also hurt my lower back before, when I slipped down a flight of aircraft steps in Belfast.

Finally, back home in Beaconsfield, where I was living at the time, my back finally seemed to collapse, with distended discs in the lower lumbar region damaging my coccyx. The hospital put me in plaster from neck to waist for some weeks, but that treatment didn't work. I could not even walk and so it was decided to operate: a laminectomy. I had to spend a month or so at Farnham Park Rehabilitation Centre, near Slough, learning to walk and run again.

CHAPTER 18

HOME AFFAIRS

Following my slow recovery from the spinal injury, I pioneered what was to become a new role in BBC News – Home Affairs Correspondent. Nobody had a clue what that was supposed to entail, only that whatever it was the BBC needed one. As things stood, stories on the home front were covered by a team of general reporters. There were correspondents for industry, economics and transport but nobody was concentrating on other areas such as health, education, immigration, police, prisons, security, all of which reflected the workings of our society. They were all very worthy, but usually lacking in glamour or headline interest. There was an unfulfilled need for a range of specialist correspondents if this territory was to be given the attention it deserved, rather than relying one person trying to cover such a broad spectrum under one umbrella.

All this came at a particularly low ebb in my life. Not only was I struggling to make sense of my new role and not feeling in the very best of health, but I was also involved in a passionate affair which was taking its toll on my home life with Gerry. To make matters worse, I was drinking heavily. In the end, though the affair finished, so did my marriage to Gerry. I moved into a bedsit in West London so I could be within walking distance of Television Centre at White City. To add insult to injury, I had also lost my driving licence after being breathalysed and found to be well over the limit.

My own self-worth took a bit of a beating during this period. I felt uncomfortable delving into the workings of the Department for Education and Science whose Secretary of State at the time was Margaret Thatcher, appointed by Edward Heath's Tory Government. For a start, with my limited formal education and no degree, I was hardly qualified to specialise in this kind of work, though at the time the BBC did not seem particularly concerned. I told them they needed at least two journalists with appropriate qualifications for the job and that their experience should include an understanding of trade unions. It was a political minefield: there were going to be some highly controversial changes under Maggie Thatcher. It was pretty obvious that she was going to be a high-flyer. She was always very friendly to me, but easily irritated by fussing ministers trying to impose their views on her. At that time, in the early 1970s, she dressed very plainly and tended to sound like an academic.

Her most striking feature were her long, slim legs. She liked dancing and at Tory Party conference times, which were also big social occasions, she would make a beeline for our cameraman, Derek Collier, a tall, broad shouldered ex-matelot, who was nimble on his feet. More interestingly he had a crush on Margaret Thatcher and she always seemed happy tripping the light fantastic with him. At the end of one interview which I recorded with her, I remember asking if she thought she would ever become Prime Minister. She smiled and said: 'There will be a woman there one day.' Five years later she was to move into Number Ten.

In my quest to define what a Home Affairs Correspondent should be doing I also looked into the workings of one the Government's biggest spenders, the Department of Health and Social Security, and almost immediately I was knee-deep in paperwork spewed out by faceless civil servants and their press office. All very worthy, but agonisingly tedious and time-consuming.

The department's saving grace, to me anyway, was that the Secretary of State for the DHSS was Barbara Castle, Socialist MP for Blackburn, who was both fiery and fun. She liked to look her best whenever she was to appear on television and seized each opportunity to have the full works. Before every interview I did with her she required that her hair be washed and styled and that a make-up artist be on hand to soften the signs of wear and tear. The session would last up to two hours. Knowing that she really enjoyed being spoiled on those occasions the BBC were happy to oblige, which at least ensured she was in a good mood when it came time to do the interview.

The work of the DHSS has an impact on all our lives. The very safety and well-being of millions of men, women and children at risk, depend upon the civil servants carrying out their responsibilities effectively. Unfortunately, through the ages there always have been those who fall below the expected standard, with somebody needing to be brought to account. I suggested there should be at least two specialist correspondents covering health and social affairs.

It was clear that the Home Office provided the most fertile ground for a Home Affairs Correspondent. Immigration, race relations, prisons, the police and homeland security would be crucial areas for the foreseeable future…a mirror, if you like, through which we might assess the progress of our increasingly multi-racial society. I soon found that the Home Office is not a comfortable environment for journalists. The trust of officials is hard-won and useful information has often to be wrung out of them. A straight answer to difficult questions, no matter how much in the public interest they might be, is so often out of reach; you would think those responsible were guarding the Crown Jewels. I still don't consider that it is in the nature of stiff, tight-lipped, English civil servants to change, especially at the Home Office where they like to give the impression that potentially everyone is against them.

Undoubtedly it is a tough job, but some strange cosmic influence seems to take over new Home Secretaries when they first walk through the door: regardless of whichever political party they represent, they start acting tough; never let your guard drop being the order of the day. Yes, Minister so successfully parodied the situation!

Famously, Michael Howard, when he was Home Secretary in the late 1970s, was asked the same question fourteen times in a live interview by Jeremy Paxman and each time he resolutely refused to answer. Prison reform was on the agenda, following a Colditz style break-out from Parkhurst top-security jail. Three killers and an arsonist had escaped and someone's head in the prison service had to roll. Paxman simply wanted to know if the security of Britain's jails ultimately rested with the Home Secretary. Yes or no? Michael Howard, poker-faced to the end, was not going to take the bait, or any blame. He tried to wriggle off the hook: it seemed as though he would rather go to his grave than give a straight answer. Paxman might just as well have been the Gestapo.

As would be expected, the police force, terrorism and race relations occupy a great deal of careful thought at the Home Office and Scotland Yard. I spent a lot of time talking to leaders among Asian and West Indian communities all over the country about racism in the police force and discrimination in employment, all of which remain sore topics today. Community leaders who gathered regularly at the Mangrove restaurant in Notting Hill would suddenly become victims of a surprise police raid. They would be falsely accused of drug-dealing and brothel-keeping. The restaurant's owner, Frank Critchlow, was constantly harassed by local police for no good reason. In my view, his place was so popular because he provided good, spicy West Indian food and great coffee; the restaurant had a really friendly atmosphere and with reggae music playing it was home from home to many West Indians, but anathema to the police.

During the Notting Hill Carnival of August 1976, tensions over the heavy presence of police in the streets exploded into the worst of the riots. Three hundred policemen were injured. I talked to community leaders that night and in ensuing days and there was general agreement that the police, though provoked, had displayed a woeful lack of understanding and knowledge of the black community they were supposed to serve. There were just too many of them, being too heavy-handed over trivial offences but, to their credit, the force eventually listened to what community leaders were telling them and policing methods were reviewed and modified. A group of officers was even sent to Trinidad to learn how the local bobbies dealt with policing the Carnival in Port-of-Spain, where the pregnancy rate and not the crime rate takes a jump during the three days of wild celebration.

The Queen, as head of the Commonwealth, was interested to hear personally how Asian and West Indian community leaders in England felt about their safety and access to opportunity. She invited a large group to Buckingham Palace for drinks and an informal chat with herself and Prince Philip. As Home Affairs Correspondent, I was also invited. Before the Queen arrived there were quite a few sceptics in the group, who couldn't see any value in the exercise. Why should the Queen really want to know, or care, about them? I have to say Her Majesty had done her homework thoroughly; by the end of the evening she had them 'eating out of her hand', because she had listened so intently to their concerns and appeared genuinely interested to learn more about what was going on at street level.

After my stint as Home Affairs Correspondent, life at the BBC opened up other opportunities for me. The producer, George Carey who was the architect of Newsnight, had finally launched the programme on BBC 2 in 1980 offering us journalists the chance to delve beyond the headlines. He had fought hard, despite the sceptics at Television Centre, to give life to a programme that is now the BBC's flagship current affairs show. Through Newsnight I was able to look into stories in much greater depth. To me it was like a breath of fresh air. Our stories were not always tied to the news of the day; if they were of public interest they could be extremely out of the ordinary, even bizarre.

Most importantly, it was George who was responsible for putting me in touch again with Rowena Scott. I had no idea that she had moved to London from Colombia and was working as secretary to the Cuban ambassador. George had attended a diplomatic function at the embassy, met Rowena and the next day he tapped me on the shoulder and gave me her telephone number, saying, 'I think you should give her a call'. I did. My reunion with Rowena would prove to be a life-changer for both of us.

Co-incidentally George, whose mother was born in Trinidad, had known Rowena since their schooldays when she was at the Priory in Haywards Heath, East Sussex. George's family lived not far away at Newick where Rowena often spent weekends with her cousin Paula Smith and her family.

After I had made that all important phone call to Rowena we started seeing a lot of each other. The spark that had drawn us together briefly, all those years ago in Trinidad, was still there and we were soon living together, at first in her tiny flat in Notting Hill and then in a beautiful Victorian maisonette in West London, which we were able to buy with a long-term fixed mortgage. They were very happy days, giving each of us a new lease of life. Rowena spread her wings and with her fluent Spanish was offered an interesting job with Amnesty International, helping political prisoners in various parts of the Spanish-speaking world.

Sometimes, through Rowena's contacts, I was given access to stories which would otherwise have remained closed. I recall being in Herez de la Frontera in Spain, trying to piece together a television feature on the British sherry industry. I needed to interview the head of the Domecq sherry family, which was proving really difficult. When I went to his factory there were hundreds of workers in the street, who had been locked out.

Nobody on the inside would open the doors to anyone, especially to the media. I phoned Rowena, who, as luck would have it, had been at school with Mercedes Domecq and I knew they still kept in touch. Rowena made a phone call to her friend and hey presto, Mercedes' father, old Domecq, ushered me and my TV crew in through a side gate.

I asked him what was going on, with all these workers thronging outside. He said: 'Last week they stopped work and had a sit-in, demanding more pay. This week I am having a lock-out'.

For the rest of the day we filmed inside his ancient bodega, a veritable history of the sherry industry with cobwebbed barrels assigned to famous names around the world: Winston Churchill, Francis Drake, Napoleon Bonaparte....

CHAPTER 19

THE ZOMBIE PHENOMENON

Zombies, as a staple ingredient of horror movies, didn't interest me much, but one evening in the Newsnight office, producer Keith Hulse handed me a piece of academic research which had been presented at a Third World conference, revealing that 'the living dead' was not a Hollywood fantasy. These unfortunates, it said, were transformed into that state as a voodoo punishment, using a secret nerve agent 160,000 times more powerful than cocaine. Normally this type of story would not be considered hard news but, if we could verify the facts, then that itself would be new and certainly worth a closer look at the bizarre world of the occult in Haiti, where this phenomenon is practised. I thought it was certainly worth investigation.

The man who had presented the paper at the conference was a doctor, little known outside his own country, called Lemarque Douyon, who ran a rehabilitation clinic for people trying to recover from zombification, in the capital, Port-au-Prince. The first problem for us would be getting into Haiti, which in the nineteen eighties was run by Papa Doc Duvalier, himself a voodooist who used his dreaded secret police, the Tons-Tons-Macoute or Bogeymen, to rule through fear. Bad publicity involving a voodoo poison, which might adversely affect the tourist industry, such as it was, would certainly not be welcome.

Dr. Douyon, whose own work in Port-au-Prince was being funded by the Rockefeller Foundation in New York, offered to fly there with some case histories of recovering zombies. Keith Hulse, went to meet him and he confirmed that there was indeed a scientific basis for the creation of zombies. We started to plan our mission: to get into Haiti, acquire samples of the zombie poison and get them tested. The success of the whole operation depended on the full and fearless co-operation of Dr. Douyon.

We flew into Haiti, via Miami, with tourist visas and a story that we were there to film the island as a holiday destination and for a few days it looked as though that was what we were doing. Security men we had seen at the airport turned up from time to time in our hotel. We had chosen the Hotel Olaffson, a nineteenth century Gingerbread-style mansion in the centre of Port-au-Prince, so that we would be visible, some of the time, to anyone spying for Papa Doc.

Over the years, the Olaffson has been made famous by the many artists and writers who have stayed there. The hotel and its lush tropical gardens was a setting for Graham Greene's 1966 novel, The Comedians. Amazingly it has remained undamaged through the years of revolution, hurricane and earthquake.

With Dr. Douyon's help we moved to different locations at night to be introduced by him to important figures in the voodoo community. Often we filmed by the light of large lamps strategically placed around a village where voodoo celebrations went on till dawn. The sound of fanatical drumming sent people into a frenzy of spirit possession. Some of the women would finish up in trees, in a trance, waving to and fro like enormous brightly-coloured birds.

One of the central figures in our investigation was Clervius Narcisse, aged 62, who had been zombified by a male voodoo priest, known as a houngan, as punishment for his part in a dispute over some land. The priest had used the native drug brought to Haiti by slaves from Africa 300 years ago. Haiti is one of the poorest countries in the world and its people are among the most super-stitious in the Caribbean. It is a country of natural beauty

Clervius Narcisse, a zombie who was rehabilitated, in Port au Prince, Haiti.

and economic ruin. Most of its eleven million people barely scratch a living from the land. For them voodoo is a way of life and an escape from the daily grind of abject poverty.

After Clervius had been poisoned his breathing deteriorated over a period of three weeks and he was pronounced dead at the Albert Schweitzer Hospital in Gonaives under the supervision of two doctors, one Haitian the other American. His death certificate said the cause was 'malignant hypertension and oedema.' But Clervius was not really dead. The drug had induced a state indistinguishable from death, numbing all his senses, except his hearing. The doctors could find no sign of a pulse, yet Clervius could hear them pronouncing him dead. He was put into a rough wooden coffin and as they nailed down the lid, one of the large nails pierced his cheek. His sister and other family members were at the graveside and a couple of weeks later they erected a tombstone there. But by then Clervius was no longer in the grave. After a long search I found his death certificate among official records in Port-au-Prince. A day after that I was talking to him, through an interpreter, in his village. On his left cheek was the scar left by the nail.

The interpreter throughout our investigation, Lilas Desquiron,

Lilas Desquiron, my dear friend and interpreter in Haiti, who opened many doors for us during this difficult investigation into the zombie poison.

was a rare find. She was born in Haiti, educated at the Sorbonne and had studied voodooism. She had a special empathy with Haitians like Clervius who had been to hell and back and they appeared at ease in her company as she drew out their story. The local Creole dialect is a melodic mixture of French and African languages as it dances off the tongue even when spoken by a zombie. His face, otherwise, expresses no emotion while his watery eyes stare yonderly at some far distant place. He is living in the moment though, answering questions about his horrific experience without hesitation. He knows he has been poisoned by a houngan, all because of an argument over a piece of land that he claimed was his. He thinks the potion was slipped into a drink. He can't remember how long he was in the coffin, probably a few hours, before he was raised from the grave by the houngan and his assistant as part of a special voodoo ceremony, without the presence of any family members. He was given an antidote, another potion which brought him out of his trance-like state, but without the ability to think and make decisions for himself. From then on, he did only what the houngan told him to do.

Clervius was put to work in the fields tending crops, in reality as a slave to his voodoo master. The kind of work zombies are given depends on the damage the nerve poison has done and how much oxygen there was in the coffin. The dosage given, though tiny, is always imprecise. Some of the victims are virtually cabbages, unable to comprehend or do anything and are just left to wander off into the forest. Clervius worked like this for years, but very slowly his mind started to clear and one day, when the houngan was shouting at him he struck the man with a spade and ran off. Police found him wandering about in distress and took him to Dr. Douyon's clinic. When his sister saw him for the first time since his funeral, she fainted.

Folklore in Haiti gives zombies special powers to seek revenge on those who brought about their demise. In the main cemetery in Port-au-Prince tombstones are chained and padlocked to deter grave robbers, such is the belief in the 'living dead.' One of Dr. Douyon's patients, Francina was given the zombie potion by a houngan following a family row in which she was accused of infidelity by her husband. The girl's mother and the jealous husband had taken the problem to the voodoo priest. We took Francina back to her village years after her funeral. People were not sure at first who the stranger in their midst was. They came out of their grass-thatched houses to peer at her walking slowly forward. Her mother and Francina's former husband came forward too, and stopped, aghast when they realised who the girl was. To us it looked as though the entire village was in a state of shock, or maybe fear. Francina moved on, through a track almost completely reclaimed by the thick forest, and stopped suddenly. The bush was cleared with a machete to reveal Francina's grave. Francina's state of mind was such that she only moved when she was directed to do so. I had forgotten that when I drove her to the village. I hopped from the car expecting her to get out of the back seat on her own but she just sat there, staring into space. I had to open the door, guide her out and tell her what to do. Returning Francina to her own graveside had no visible impact on her whatsoever.

For so long the academic cognoscenti in the western world had rejected the notion of a zombie poison out of hand, consigning it to black magic, unworthy of scientific respectability. As far back as 1803, slaves in what was the French West Indian colony of San Domingo 'poisoned' much of Napoleon Bonaparte's army over a period of time and finally revolted under the leadership of Toussaint L'Ouverture to establish the Negro state of Haiti. It was the only successful slave revolt in history.

French slave traders had captured entire villages in West Africa and the Congo, including "witch doctors" who possessed generations of knowledge about the plant and fish life in their region. The secrets of the zombie poison tended to be kept within the family of the houngan, then handed down from father to son. Not everyone professing to be a houngan in Haiti today is genuine. There are charlatans who go through elaborate performances for tourists, providing a spooky atmosphere set to the sound of frantic drumming, maybe even walking barefoot over hot coals. But the genuine guardians of the formula for creating zombies are not interested in sharing their secrets for money. They are even reluctant to make the knowledge available for scientific scrutiny.

Dr. Douyon, who was educated at MacGill University in Montreal, made it possible for the first time to analyse samples of the genuine formula and study some genuine cases of zombification. The samples we collected from four widely-separated localities in Central and Northern Haiti were sealed in special canisters we had brought with us from England. In each case we watched the houngan, wearing a face-mask soaked in lemon juice, prepare the concoction: the saliva and heart from a large toad or bufo, shavings from the shinbone of a male skeleton which he dug up in a cemetery and the entrails of a puffer fish. These gastronomic delights were then boiled up in an iron cooking pot. They were finally dried and made into a powder.

At this point you are probably thinking: what a load of rubbish. Well, so was I. None of the houngans would explain their chosen ingredients in any meaningful detail, which made me even more sceptical. Maybe they preferred to camouflage the real secret of their recipe like a top chef protecting his piece de resistance. The important thing, as Dr. Douyon impressed upon me, was that we now had samples which would enable us to find out for ourselves, one way or the other.

When I went through Miami airport with my precious canisters a customs officer insisted that I open them. I told him briefly what they contained and that they were destined for Professor Schultes at Harvard University's laboratories. I showed him a letter from the Professor and said that if he opened them he should wear a face mask for safety, in case any fumes were toxic. I refused to open them myself. He paused momentarily, then waved me through.

It was Professor Schultes who discovered the nerve agent curare, used by natives in blow-pipes to neutralise prey in the Amazon jungle. In the laboratory at Harvard he worked with a young ethno-biologist, Wade Davis, on the samples we had brought back from Haiti. They finally told us that the main nerve agent in the zombie potion was Tetrodotoxin which was to be found in its most concentrated form in the ovaries, liver and intestines of a particular type of puffer fish, Diodon Holocanthus, most prevalent in the Caribbean and South China Sea. The female of the species was more dangerous. Puffers are so-called because of their ability to inflate themselves for protection by swallowing water when they are frightened. Despite the risks of eating it the puffer fish is a delicacy in Japanese cuisine, known as fugu. People still occasionally die from it despite the licensing of specially-trained fugu chefs by the Japanese government. Traces of tetrodotoxin are particularly strong in the female's ovaries during her reproductive period, while the male's testicles are tasty but innocuous. Deaths in Japan have occurred because the chef has been unable to distinguish an ovary from a testicle. There are cases of fugu poisoning when the customer, rendered comatose, has been presumed dead, but made a miraculous recovery later inside a coffin en route to the cemetery.

In the laboratory Wade Davis tried the tetrodotoxin samples on the skin of aggressive apes and within minutes they were completely comatose though their mental faculties were working. They were oblivious to pain. He likened their condition to an animal going into hibernation. In a human, he said, the drug destroys that part of the brain which governs speech and will-power, so the victim cannot formulate thought. He and his associates said the plants and parts of the frog used in the zombie potion were hallucinogenic, but Tetrodotoxin was the most active by far – 160,000 times more effective than cocaine. Hard to believe.

After our investigation in Haiti the BBC sold the film in fifty-six countries. An Australian TV channel which had bought the film wanted to make their own version to give a new woman presenter a good launch. They asked me to give them the names of all the contacts I had made and the locations of all the places we'd managed to film. I refused. A few months later I was told that they had gone to Haiti anyway, had their camera equipment smashed, and were forced to leave the country.

Wade Davis went to Haiti on the back of our research and befriended the daughter of one of the houngans. They had an affair and he promised to help her with a higher education in America. In return she gave him the entrée to her voodoo world. The result was a book, 'The Serpent and the Rainbow' and a B-movie horror story which enabled him to buy a house back home. That did not go down at all well in Port-au-Prince. He told me all about it a year later when I met him in London. He looked so thin and gaunt, not at all the healthy, chunky guy I had known.

"I made a big mistake," he said, "and I can never go back to Haiti."

Following the film he had returned to Haiti with his French girlfriend in tow. They met the houngan and the girl to whom he had promised so much. Soon after he left Haiti his health began to fail and he felt he might die.

"I have been in and out of hospital for most of the year," he said. "I think her father wanted to teach me a lesson."

CHAPTER 20

GOLDFINGER

Very occasionally, on current affairs programmes such as Newsnight, it is considered permissible to dramatise certain sequences if it helps to explain the story effectively, without distorting the facts. There was a case at the Old Bailey in the nineteen eighties in which the nine people in the dock were accused of swindling the Inland Revenue out of forty-two million pounds in VAT on imported gold bullion. The two men who had master-minded the scam had escaped abroad.

At that time, there was a loophole in the law which gave companies trading in gold six months in which to pay the VAT. The 'Goldfinger' gang used this to get rich quickly. It was a Customs and Excise case which would be anything but quick; it was going to take many weeks in court to unravel the weary arithmetic of the fraud. Using the evidence to turn the case into a watchable television programme was not going to be an easy task, so the producer Dave Rowley and I decided to use actors to play the roles of 'cops and robbers.' Anything they had to say was taken from the actual evidence. We had a good relationship with the Customs investigators who had worked so hard to crack the case and they agreed to give us access to everything they had on the strict understanding that none of their information would be broadcast until the case at the Bailey had ended. So, as the case continued, we pieced together our future film.

The gang started by setting up six companies which would 'disappear' before the VAT on gold became due in six months. They bought a few ingots to begin with and flew them into London from Zurich by British Airways. Each day, when the price of gold was fixed on the London Bullion Market, the gang would offer their legally imported bars for sale at slightly below the market value to Asian jewellers in London, knowing that they would jump at the bargain. The court had named the two men behind the scam, who were still at large somewhere in the world. They also gave out several aliases one of the men had used. A customs official had told me that during a house search a postcard had been found from Fuengirola, an area of southern Spain which had become known as La Costa del Crime. There was no extradition treaty in place with Britain and so criminals used it as a bolthole. With the trial still promising a long way to run, it was well worth a flight to Spain.

Fuengirola was a busy cosmopolitan town on the coast, popular among Brits with some savings to spend; small apartments were cheap. For the super-rich and the two men who had escaped were certainly in that league, there were elegant homes with gardens and swimming pools hidden away in the hills above the town. We were told of a small village where British estate agents specialised in these properties. In fact, apart from six agents, the place had little more than a convenience store to offer alongside a string of donkeys which people could hire to explore the countryside. I tried all the agents, asking whether any Englishman had recently bought a really big property, with a view of the Mediterranean. First, I gave them the names of the two fraudsters at large. Nothing came up on their computers. I then tried the aliases: the fifth one produced a result. The agent gave me the address and off I went.

The property must have cost several million euros. I entered through double iron gates and walked up to a large, white-stone, single-storey house with a wide verandah around it, overlooking an oblong pool looking out over the glistening Mediterranean. An elderly couple with south London accents came to the door. I guessed they were probably the parents of one of the missing men. Neither of them were home, they said and they didn't know when they'd be back. I explained who I was and showed them my BBC identity card, because I didn't want to scare them into thinking I might really be a British policeman posing as a reporter. I told them not to worry and that I would come back later, which I did after about an hour. On that second visit they said I should contact a lawyer they'd hired in Fuengirola. There had been a bit of 'bovver' and he was sorting it out. The lawyer was rather more forthcoming. He told me both his clients were in Malaga Jail accused of assault. Apparently, they had trusted a local accountant, an English resident, with a very large amount of money to deposit in a Swiss bank but he had helped himself to some of it, to buy a smart new car. So, they roughed him up a bit and threatened worse if he didn't pay the money back. The man had then staggered down the road and reported them to the Guardia Civil. Shortly afterwards both were arrested. They were now awaiting a hearing before local magistrates.

Originally, I thought that we might end our film with the two men who'd escaped trial in London lounging by their pool in Spain, sipping champagne and putting two fingers up to the law. Now it had become more complicated. Dave Rowley and I went to see the governor of Malaga Jail, to enquire if we might film our two villains. He looked at us incredulously. No-one from the media ever came into his prison, especially with cameras; absolutely out of the question. 'De ninguna manner, senor.' Only the Ministry of the Interior in Madrid could give that kind of permission. I told him I would try a contact I had made and hopefully come back later if that was OK. The governor didn't look too impressed.

I had covered a number of stories in Spain, over the years, including some from the Basque country during ETA's separatist bombing campaign. My main military contact at that time was now in the Ministry of the Interior in Madrid. I told my colleague, Dave Rowley, that it was a long shot, but this particular contact had promised me that if ever I needed help I was to ring him. My experience in Spain is that most people are honourable and if they do make a promise, they stick to it. Dave didn't look too optimistic either but I made the call, all the same.

Fortunately the contact was pleased to hear from me and I explained why I needed access to the jail. I felt that because it involved two British criminals, it was of no great importance to Madrid and in a way, the villains were getting what they deserved. My contact felt that, in this case, it would be alright for us to enter the prison and to film the two men. He would inform the local prison governor immediately and that is exactly what happened. My colleague was amazed. The governor was also more than a little surprised when we returned to his office.

He said: 'Madrid has given permission; so, get your equipment and follow me.' No-one was more startled to see a film crew than our two villains, when their cell door was opened and they were brought into the exercise yard. The governor told them who we were but they were convinced that the whole thing was a set-up: we were really from Scotland Yard and that there was a car waiting outside to whisk them down the road forty-eight miles to Gibraltar and onto a waiting plane back to London and the Old Bailey, to join their friends in the dock. There was a lot of loud cursing as I tried to explain that we were no threat to them; all they had to worry about was the assault case before the local magistrates. There was no extradition treaty with Spain so they could not be extradited to England. They had got away with the gold bullion swindle.

Eventually they calmed down and started to take an interest in how we'd pieced the film together. Finally, they invited us to go back to their grand house when they got out of the jail, so we could raise a glass or two by the pool. When our jailhouse filming was over and we were back outside, Dave Rowley was ecstatic. 'Bloody Hell,' he said. 'Nobody will ever believe this. What an ending.'

CHAPTER 21

THE HUNTER AND THE HUNTED

The train robber Ronnie Biggs had been on the run for nine years since his escape from Wandsworth Prison in 1965, while serving a thirty-year sentence. He had been located, at last, in Rio de Janeiro, Brazil. Most of his share of the £2.6 million heist, £40 million in today's money, had dwindled away. The Daily Express had offered him a large sum of money for his story and kept him in hiding somewhere. Nevertheless, the rest of Fleet Street and just about everyone else in the media, including the BBC, wanted to talk to him.

Just before the story broke, Detective Chief Superintendent Jack Slipper of Scotland Yard had flown out to Brazil to arrest him, but had to return empty-handed because of a legal technicality. It was a big embarrassment. How was he to know that Ronnie had become the father of a Brazilian child and so, under local law, could not be extradited.

I really felt sorry for Jack when he told me what had happened. He had flown across the Atlantic with Detective Inspector Peter Jones. They had downed a few drinks on the plane, as you do, and weren't feeling so good when they landed and headed for the federal police headquarters for back up. Neither of them understood a word of Portuguese, but with the help of a British consular official, they had managed to explain that they were going to arrest a British citizen for a serious robbery in England and enquired whether a couple of local policemen might come with them to an address they had been given. It was the hotel room of Express reporter Colin Mackenzie and his photographer Bill Lovelace who were in hiding there with Ronnie Biggs, unravelling his story. The Scotland Yard men were counting on the element of surprise. They had no official power in Brazil; neither the Home Office nor the Foreign Office had been informed of their trip.

The room was on the third floor, Jack told me. They did not want to get stuck in a lift, so we went up the stairs. Jack knocked on the door. Ronnie was taken by surprise, but he was not going to make any trouble. He just didn't want to be taken away in handcuffs. The Brazilian cops didn't like this soft approach and one of them produced a revolver.

Ronnie was not pleased. Jack said, 'Oh Great! This is all we need.' Ronnie didn't trust the Brazilians not to shoot him, calling the cop with the gun a son of a bitch and telling him, in Portuguese that if he didn't put his 'shooter' away he'd stick it right up his arse. Of course, that changed everything. The Brazilian policemen were about to get tough, but Jack stepped in and calmed everyone down, telling Ronnie he'd just have to hang onto his trouser belt. No need for cuffs. Ronnie seemed OK with that, so Jack told them that they would stop off at his flat on the way to the nick to pick up some warm clothes. It was going to be bloody cold in England.

Our two Scotland Yard officers had thought that all would go without a hitch. They had booked a seat for Ronnie on a plane back to London. Now Ronnie, who had been ready to accompany them, was behind bars. He got talking to a local man in the cell, who explained that if he had a Brazilian wife or girlfriend and they had a baby he could not be extradited. Ronnie and his Amerindian girlfriend, Raimunda had a son, Michael. It was now a different story. Ronnie asked to see a lawyer. He was going nowhere, certainly not with Detective Chief Superintendent Jack Slipper. In the British newspapers there was a picture of an empty seat between the two British detectives as they returned to London. Ronnie, once again, was free, though his continued residence in Rio was due to be settled in the local family court. His big problem was that he had entered Brazil with a forged passport under the name of Mick Haynes, which was how his local friends knew him until the real story broke.

By now Ronnie had come to suspect that it was the Daily Express all along who had tipped off Scotland Yard in London because, not content with locating him after all these years, they wanted the story of his capture as well. I reached Rio de Janeiro, with producer Gordon Carr and a TV crew, not knowing where Ronnie Biggs was still in hiding. I knew he was a carpenter by trade, so I reckoned he would have found work somewhere, to make a little money. Most of his share of the train robbery £147,000, some £2.5 million in today's currency, had gone by now. I guessed that if Ronnie needed to advertise his trade skills in Rio he would try the English language newspaper. It was through the newspaper that we discovered that Ronnie was doing a lot of work at the home of an American family. We decided that if we got to know any of the people Ronnie saw regularly we would eventually get to him and that's the way it happened.

An American family of Christian Scientists, the Hubers, had become fond of Ronnie who was making their kitchen furniture. Whenever their two children asked him what he did in England he said: 'I was a train robber.' Of course they all took it as a joke. Through a tight group of his English-speaking friends and employers Ronnie learned that someone from the BBC wanted to talk to him. After the incident with Jack Slipper I knew that he had to report regularly to a local police station, which is where we eventually came face to face. He was a tall, handsome man, following facial surgery in Europe, with smiling eyes, very relaxed. When I told him I wanted to interview him he asked, at once, how much I was willing to pay.

I had to be honest with him. 'You may laugh,' I said, 'but I'm afraid the best the BBC can do is twenty-five pounds.'

He laughed outright. 'People are offering me tens of thousands, mate,' he said.

I laughed too saying, 'Puts me at a bit of a disadvantage, doesn't it, but the BBC has this policy of not paying large sums of money to criminals.'

I'd taken a gamble, but he was amused and looked at me as though I must be completely naïve or off my head. I gave him an outline of the story we'd planned to do with him and asked him to consider it. 'You may actually enjoy it,' I said, giving him my hotel number. He walked away, smiling. I only half expected to see him again.

A couple of days later Ronnie walked into my hotel. 'Let's talk,' he said. 'I'm getting a bit bored with the Express.' In reality the newspaper had got their story. It had been a world scoop. Now they were trying to keep him out of reach of the rest of the media, to defeat their competition.

Ronnie was an engaging, charismatic character with a nut-brown Copacabana tan. He loved the easy beach life, local food, dancing the samba and a good spliff. Most importantly he loved his son, Michael, who had shot to fame by now in a boy band, Balao Magico, which had started to bring in lots of money, enabling them to buy a big house in Rio, not far from the sea front at Copacabana beach. We did a few recordings on tape about his involvement in the robbery. The first one was a hoot: he was completely stoned, so we scrapped it.

Ronnie had been a late addition to the train robbery gang. His old friend, Bruce Reynolds, who had planned the job, had offered him 'a piece of the business'. One of the highlights of the evening's work, he said, was counting the money in the kitchen at the farmhouse they had rented. The cash was piled up to the ceiling and they were playing monopoly with it when there was a knock at the door. Bruce Reynolds went to see who it was.

Ronnie said: 'It was the local bobby who wanted to know if it would be alright for a friend to graze his horse in one of the fields next to the farm. Bruce calmly gave his permission and invited the cop in for a drink. I nearly had a heart attack. What the hell was he thinking?' The village policeman politely turned down the offer ....'Maybe another time, sir, when I'm off duty.' Back in the kitchen everyone breathed again.

A lifetime had passed since that night in August 1963, when the gang had stopped the Glasgow to London train carrying one hundred and twenty-four sacks of untraceable old notes on the way to be incinerated. Ronnie had escaped to Australia, where he had lived with his wife Charmian and their two children until 1970, when the police were on his tail again: he was forced to say farewell to them, this time taking a boat bound for South America..

There was a media frenzy in Rio, with newspapers all trying to snatch him from the clutches of the Daily Express, if they could find him, that is. Our idea was to book a studio at Brazil's TV Globo, sneak him in there, not to be interviewed by me, but to be confronted by his old adversary, Slipper of the Yard.

We would phone the famous detective in London and ask him to go to the TV Centre in Wood lane. The public could then watch the Hunter and the Hunted talk to each other on a satellite link-up about the highs and lows of what was one of the most audacious robberies of the century. Fleet Street couldn't possibly match that. All went well, until the BBC decided that it was an unacceptable gimmick; Biggs was a good talker and might glamorise the life he had led on the run, giving the impression that crime really paid. The whole idea was dropped. I couldn't believe it, neither could Ronnie and neither could my old Fleet Street colleagues when I told them later what a narrow escape they'd had.

A few years later, I was back in Rio on a harrowing story about the plight of Brazil's street children and so I called on Ronnie. Over lunch he told me that when Jack Slipper retired from Scotland Yard he had invited him to come to Rio for a well-earned holiday, all expenses paid. Jack had jumped at the chance and the two of them spent a week on the town. I asked Ronnie why the hell he hadn't phoned me. The meeting would have made an exciting television piece.'

For a long time, Ronnie had missed being in London. The old gang had finished their sentences. He thought, if he returned, the authorities might be lenient with him, although I told him it was very unlikely. He regretted that the train driver, Jack Mills, had been coshed during the robbery; 'That was not supposed to happen,' he said. In the end Ronnie did return to the UK and was committed to Belmarsh Prison. He was given hospital treatment for leukaemia and released on compassionate grounds in 2009.

Chief Superintendent Jack Slipper died in 2001, aged 81. Ronnie died in a care home in 2013, aged 84.

CHAPTER 22

ONE WOMAN'S WAR

A warm Mediterranean breeze caresses the parade ground to the sound of a brass band playing the regimental song of the French Foreign Legion. Among those being decorated for courage and bravery under fire is one woman, standing to attention in front of an entire brigade of war-hardened Legionnaires: she is tall, slim, pin-smart in her khaki uniform, enjoying one of the proudest moments of her life as two medals are pinned to the left side of her jacket – the Croix de Guerre and the Ordre du

Legionnaire Susan Travers during a quiet moment in the desert war against Rommel. The picture was sent to me by my friend and colleague Pierre Haneuse of the BBC French Service.

Corps Armé. She is the only woman ever to become a legionnaire and not by deception or disguise, but the hard way…in battle. Her name is Susan Travers, the daughter of a retired British army officer. On the legionnaires Roll of Honour at Aubagne, their headquarters near Marseilles, she is listed simply as S. Travers: 22166.

My friend Pierre Haneuse, formerly from the French Service at the BBC, uncovered this gem of a story about Susan during his research into Legion history. As we travel to her home, twelve miles to the east of Paris, neither of us knows what is in store for us. It is a modest little house with a dusty, dented, old Citroen parked alongside. Susan herself is charming, comfortably dressed and very feminine, although one of the first things she tells us is that she wishes she had been born a boy. She was happiest on the sports field, particularly on the tennis court where she'd won quite a few trophies: she seems to have played in tennis tournaments all over Europe, including Budapest, Vienna, St. Moritz and Paris.

Although she lives in modest comfort now, she had been born into a wealthy upper-class military family, spent her childhood in Devon and Cannes, before being sent to finishing school in Florence. It was a privileged existence, enjoying the hospitality of friends in smart homes and hotels across the continent. But she craved real adventure.

Susan puts on the kettle and over tea and cake in her small sitting room, she lays out the blood and guts of her story; there is no sense of drama in her voice, but modest pride in being part of the Legion's stand against Rommel, the Desert Fox, in 1942.

Susan, who was a fluent French speaker and had trained as a nurse, was eager to find an interesting job with the British army but found that all the best ones had been taken. By now Italy had joined Germany against the Allies. The French government had capitulated but split the country in two. At a meeting in the spa town of Vichy, in the unoccupied sector of France, the Commander-in-Chief of the French Army, Marshal Petain, agreed to form an Administration that would support Hitler. With swastikas fluttering in Paris, the French Secretary of State for War, General Charles de Gaulle, who had the backing of Winston Churchill, fled to London to form the Free French Army to fight against the Nazis and the so-called 'Vichy' government.

With Britain now in Hitler's sights, Susan sailed for England and at the suggestion of her wealthy aunt in Kensington, decided to knock on General de Gaulle's door in Carlton Gardens in the heart of London. It was a hive of activity. French officers subjected her to very close questioning about her motives and were impressed by her forthrightness and positive approach to war. She could easily have found work in the women's land army or in a hospital, but she wanted to prove that she could withstand the pressures of the battlefront as well as any man, though she knew nothing of the desert warfare that would be awaiting her in North Africa.

The French were happy to take her. She was given a full medical and told to equip herself for duty in the tropics. From the Army and Navy store in Victoria she bought a canvas fold-up bed, a canvas bath and the clothes she thought she would need. Just over a week later, with Hitler's bombardment of Britain taking its toll, she set sail from Liverpool with General de Gaulle's entourage, bound for Africa. Their mission was to persuade the French colonies under Vichy pro-German control, to stand up to the Nazis by joining the Free French.

Finally, they were to link up with the French Foreign Legion in North Africa. One of the two ships leaving Liverpool, flying the Cross of Lorraine, the emblem of the Free French, carried a thousand newly recruited Legionnaires. The ships were escorted by British battleships and a brand-new aircraft carrier, the Ark Royal, with its two RAF squadrons.

In Africa, the legendary German officer, General Erwin Rommel, had taken overall command in order to strengthen the resolve of the Italian forces on his side: his Afrika Korps in Libya were already tipping the balance in the Nazi's favour. His strategy was to drive the British and their allies out of Egypt completely and into the sea. After one battle he recorded in his diary that 'the Germans had faced the toughest British resistance imaginable, but by early afternoon, the whole position was ours. British resistance was quenched. We took in all three thousand prisoners and destroyed or captured one hundred and one tanks and armoured cars as well as a hundred and twenty-four guns of all kinds.'

Rommel gained the first initiative in that encounter, but the war in north Africa was far from over. The Allies needed time to regroup south-west of Tobruk, near Libya's border with Egypt. Churchill was getting impatient to turn the tide against Rommel and sent General Montgomery to restructure the Eighth Army. As Monty had to gain time, in order to plan the massive counter-attack, the French Foreign Legion was needed to provide back-up and to play a pivotal role in gaining the required breathing space.

Four thousand legionnaires, commanded by General Marie-Pierre Koenig, were positioned at the most southerly point of the British line of resistance – the Gaza Line which ran nearly one hundred and fifty miles from the coastal town of El Gazala near Tobruk across the desert to Bir Hakeim. British sappers had laid minefields in a series of boxes along the route protecting each defensive position. If Rommel could be tempted to smash his way through these formidable defences, he would run headlong into Montgomery's Eighth Army, the Desert Rats, who were ready and waiting for him. His alternative would be to go round the defences by taking the longer route to the south: and there the Legion at Bir Hakeim would come into action.

Susan told us that Bir Hakeim was a hell hole, like an oven, with daytime temperatures around 120 degrees Fahrenheit. There was no oasis, as the name suggests, just the remains of an Italian fort on an ancient camel train route from the Sahara.

The encampment was almost entirely underground, in a system of dug-outs. Only the Red Cross and mess tents were visible to German aircraft. The legionnaires had dug a shelter for Susan close to General Koenig's quarters, with just enough room for her camp bed and a little table. During her time with the Legion, Susan had been careful to make it clear that she wasn't there to flirt with battle-hardened warriors, who were respectful. Nevertheless she had formed an intimate relationship with both General Koenig and also with a charismatic Colonel Dimitri Amilakvari, a white Russian prince, who had fled the Bolshevik Revolution and had also joined the Legion. She told us that she hadn't allowed herself to fall in love with him, although he was the sort of man she had been looking for all her life. Both men protected her, but in Bir Hakeim with battle looming, there was no opportunity for a love affair to bloom with either man.

The French Foreign Legion counter-attack Rommel's desert forces during the battle of Bir Hakeim.

As the General's driver had been killed by a mine, he appointed Susan to take his place: she had already proved to him that she could keep her nerve under pressure. On a moonlight night in May, Rommel made his move. His Afrika Korps was suddenly on Bir Hakeim's doorstep. Susan retreated to her dug-out and crammed a tin helmet onto her head as the barrage from his tanks began. Rommel had told Hitler that the Legion would not be much of an obstacle and that he should be able to sweep them aside in fifteen minutes, but the minutes ran into hours, days, then weeks and despite heavy shelling and aerial bombardment the Legionnaires kept fighting back.

They had enclosed their outpost within a minefield known as The Box and would thread their way out at night using a secret route, to continue the fight at close quarters, knocking out tanks with explosives. The Germans dropped fifteen hundred shells on the Legion's garrison killing or wounding many of the legionnaires. However, the main strength of Koenig's men was that wherever they came from, whatever they had done in the past, they owed their allegiance to the Legion. It was their home, their family and war only tightened that bond. They were fighting for the honour of the Legion which had offered them sanctuary and anonymity when they needed it most. Appropriately, the Legion's motto is 'Legio Patria Nostra'; The Legion is our Country.

Stuka dive-bombers strafed the compound day after day. The hospital tent was full of holes, but still Legionnaires would come out of their hiding places to knock out tanks with grenades and Molotov cocktails. Inside the encampment ammunition and water was running out. They were living on tinned rations. Susan kept having to dig the General's car out of the sand after each heavy bombardment.

Finally, Rommel sent a message to the legionnaires to cease their resistance and run up a white flag, or they would be exterminated. General Koenig told him to go to hell; for the Legion surrender was not an option. Rommel continued his onslaught for a week. Despite the Red Crosses being clearly visible, shells hit the tents, killing some of the wounded. Medicines were destroyed. The legionnaires were now down to a cupful of water a day. The situation was hopeless. General Koenig sent a message to the Eighth Army that the show was almost over. Bir Hakeim was surrounded. 'Long Live Free France.' The General then told Susan that the Legion was going to break out through enemy lines the following evening. It would be at midnight when, hopefully, the enemy was sleeping. Soft lights pointing downward would show them the way through the minefield and legionnaires would move forward on foot.

General Koenig, with Susan at the wheel of his jeep, would lead the rest of the convoy with Amilakvari and his men bringing up the rear. Trucks carrying the seriously wounded would follow once the path through the minefield had been safely found. When the time came the troops moved slowly, silently ahead. All was going well until a machine-gun carrier strayed off the path and exploded a mine. Suddenly the entire

139

minefield was illuminated with German flares. The Legionnaires at the front launched themselves at the heavy guns only to be cut down by raking fire. Amilakvari's vehicle was blown into the air, but somehow he escaped unscathed and rallied his men to prepare for hand-to-hand fighting. The General shouted at Susan to put her foot down and try to avoid the shell holes. Amilakvari jumped in beside them with his Thompson sub-machine gun. They were supposed to be heading for a British position about forty miles away to the north, but in the midst of such mayhem and carnage there was no time to take a compass reading and a fog now descended, making the track ahead a complete blur. With the thin light of dawn, the fog started to lift, revealing the northern star, but they could neither see nor hear any of the convoy behind them. General Koenig was berating himself for having risked the lives of so many people with a mass break-out.

The General's car was full of bullet holes. Several had gone through the seats in which they were sitting. With amazing good luck they arrived alive at the British rallying point, where nobody had heard any news from Bir Hakeim. After a few hours, the ragged survivors of the convoy came into view across the desert, including the walking wounded. The General and Amilakviri were in tears: while some two thousand four hundred men made it, nearly a thousand were missing, presumed dead.

The legionnaires of Bir Hakeim were sent to Cairo for a rest and to receive the personal thanks of General de Gaulle, who flew in to present medals to Amilakviri and Pierre Messmer, a legionnaire officer who was later to become Prime Minister of France. He and his company were the last to leave Bir Hakeim and had to fight every inch of the way. Susan got her medals later. When Rommel finally punched his way into Bir Hakeim he was amazed to find it empty. Later he wrote: 'Seldom in Africa was I given such a hard-fought struggle'.

Montgomery toured his battle lines in final preparation of the planned counter-attack, which was to end in the epic victory at El Alamein. He had told his men that they would be expected to fight to the death. Two battalions of the Foreign Legion were ordered to mount an attack on a well-fortified enemy position at El Himeimat, on top of a sheer cliff face. Amilakviri called it madness but he was unaware that Montgomery intended the

Legion's assault to be a diversionary tactic, to keep enemy forces busy while the main attack took place further to the north-east. The legionnaires were trapped and heavily blasted by the guns of German Panzers and the Italian Ariete divisions. Amilakviri was killed by a piece of shrapnel which entered his throat and went out through his head. He never wore a tin helmet in battle, only his legionnaire's tepi. As he used to say: 'Death Knows When It's Your Time.'

Susan continued her service with the Legion throughout the war in Europe and later in Vietnam. She eventually married a legionnaire sergeant, Nicholas Schlegelmich, four years her junior. He was nothing like her Russian Prince, Amilakviri, or her General Koenig, but he was a loyal, kind, passionate man. They had been very happy in retirement until his death from liver cancer in 1995. A year later Susan was awarded the Legion d'Honneur ... the French Foreign Legion's highest military medal. She had become a legend in her own time.

CHAPTER 23

THE HOLY WAR

Occasionally I was asked by friends: where do you start when told to go and cover a war? BBC TV News rarely gave us much time to plan anything and what you did was left entirely up to you. That was certainly the case in the early 1980s at the start of the Iran-Iraq war. For a start there was the tedious inquisition at the Iraqi embassy in London before they agreed to give you a visa. The war made it impossible to fly directly to Baghdad or anywhere else in Iraq, so the nearest point of entry was Amman, Jordan. I looked at the map: there was one narrow road wending its way across the Syrian Desert, a distance of over five hundred and sixty miles.

We had taken just enough basic equipment to camp out for a few nights, including a primus stove, tinned food, water and a small pan. It was early evening when we reached Amman and we were keen to get moving on our trek across the desert to take advantage of the cool evening temperature. At this stage our knowledge of what was going on in the war was pretty basic and we knew nothing of any danger we might encounter on the way across the vast empty space. We had taken with us plenty of American dollars, knowing that the local Arabs would always be happy to accept that currency. We could not find any local taxi driver prepared to make the long journey and finally decided to buy an old grey bus which, we were assured, would make it across the desert, with a couple extra jerry cans of water. I wouldn't have taken the chance in normal circumstances, but, in times of war, you're sometimes left with a wing and a prayer.

Several times in the night, under an amazing galaxy of stars, we pulled off the sand-blown road to make tea. We usually stopped alongside a group of Bedouin tribesmen, huddled beside their camels. I reckoned that if it was safe for them to stop it would probably be alright for us too. It was an interesting sight – men from two completely different cultures taking tea in their own particular way. Their method was simple but much more elaborate. They travelled with dry kindling and large stones with which they made a fire. The stones were arranged to take a pan in which they poured their tea leaves, water and copious amounts of sugar. No words were exchanged between us, they were just as interested in the way we boiled our tea on a primus stove as we were in their customs. They did seem amused by the sight of our old bus and I wondered what they were really thinking … what a bunch of idiots, perhaps.

It was early dawn when we eventually reached the still outskirts of Baghdad in our bus, smoke now beginning to escape

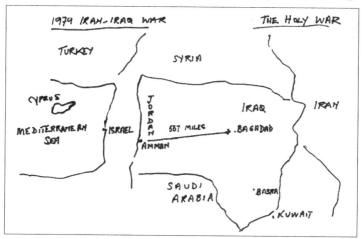

During my covering the Iran-Iraq war in 1979 we made a 567-mile road journey through the desert from Amman in Jordan to Baghdad.

from beneath the bonnet, having guzzled all our remaining water. We just made it to the hotel designated for us by the Iraqi military official in London. Only then did I have time to read the pile of newspaper cuttings I had brought and bring myself up to date with the background to this holy war.

That same evening I made my way up to the roof of the hotel which had a great view of the beautiful, sprawling city. Someone had warned me: be careful. I could see anti-aircraft guns around a military compound next to the hotel, otherwise the scene was quiet. It seemed as though there was no war going on at all. Then suddenly, out of nowhere, a surface-to-surface missile appeared metres below me heading straight along the street to find its target – an Iraqi command post down the road, which just disappeared in the blast. Immediately I was made

143

aware that the technology of warfare was changing fast. I hurried downstairs and carried on with my homework, briefing myself on how this clash of neighbouring states had come about.

In 1979 the Shah of Iran, Mohammad Reza Pahlavi, had gone into exile and Ayatollah Khomeini was leading the country's Islamic Revolution. He vowed to avenge Shia victims of Baathist repression in neighbouring Iraq and called on the population there to rise up against the leader of the ruling Sunni minority, Saddam Hussein.

For his part, Hussein already feared that Tehran's new leadership of the Shia might trigger that revolt and decided to exploit Iran's post-revolutionary vulnerability himself. He knew that despite the Shah's stockpile of the latest weapons, the new regime had executed or driven all of its top military personnel into exile, some twelve thousand senior officers. As a result of Khomeini's purge, the Iranian Air Force was only able to fly half of its aircraft. His Revolutionary Guard was led by clerics with no military experience. So, by 1980 Saddam Hussein was at war, hoping for a swift victory. He also had a strategic reason for fighting: he wanted full sovereignty of the Shatt-al-Arab waterway in the south, Iraq's only access to the Persian Gulf.

Early in the eight-year war with Iran, Saddam Hussein insisted that all visiting journalists be housed in the brand-new Al Rasheed Hotel in Baghdad. His government would pick up the bill, but that way his security men could keep an eye on reporters' movements. Official information concerning the war effort would be handed out at daily meetings. The problem was we couldn't believe a word of it. Repeated attempts to visit the front, to see for ourselves what was really going on, were blocked. On the few occasions that Saddam's henchmen organised trips to bombed villages, it seemed to me that the places had been sanitised before any of us got there, to give the impression that the Iranian Air Force wasn't really very good at its job; there were never any Iraqi residents whom we might interview.

Saddam went to great lengths to use the foreign media for his propaganda. He would have us believe that the war with Iran would be a quick one. Life in the capital, Baghdad, would go on almost as normal. True, the eighteen storey Al Rasheed Hotel was spacious and plush; according to the publicity it was destined to become the most luxurious in the world, second only to the Waldorf Astoria in New York City. Saddam had used billions of dollars in loans from Saudi Arabia to improve Iraq's infrastructure and build a new modern airport, but now the billions were going into his war effort.

Strangely, Bagdad seemed to be trapped somewhere between Nuremburg in pre-war Germany and modern-day Las Vegas. There were huge portraits of Saddam everywhere in the streets with martial music booming from TV sets and speakers and yet there were girls in tight jeans and colourful blouses, in stark contrast to the full hijab in Iran; nightclubs were still open and restaurants selling liquor. Baghdad seemed to be screened from the realities of the war going on only one hundred and fifty

Myself in Iraq.

miles away. People I met who lived in the suburbs of Baghdad did not want to talk openly about the fighting. If you supported Saddam, you were expected to lay down your life for him and there were those who really did see him as their saviour. He could do no wrong. To them, stories of Sadam ordering the massacre of thousands of his own people were foreign lies. On the other hand, if you did not support Saddam then you kept your views to yourself, if you wanted to keep your head.

I delivered some mail from an Iraqi friend working at the BBC in London to her family, who lived in a quiet residential road in Baghdad, but they were uneasy about my being seen visiting them. Neighbours would gossip, especially about white foreigners and if it was the wrong kind of gossip there would be repercussions. They knew of people who had reported neighbours for speaking ill of Saddam and they had just disappeared. We were told that soldiers returning from the front had been forbidden to talk negatively about their experiences, for fear of casting a shadow over the way the troops were being treated. There were occasional Iranian bombing raids on the capital at this early stage of the war, but they didn't appear to have much impact on the city or on its commercial operations.

By now, Rowena and I were engaged to be married. From my room at the Rasheed Hotel, I had been trying for days to get a call through to her in London. One night, right in the middle of an air raid, I was on the roof watching the fireworks with the phone in my pocket when it rang. Rowena wanted to know what the hell was going on, so I was able to give her a running commentary on the Iranian Phantom jets that were strafing the area around us. With anti-aircraft guns blazing away below and searchlights criss-crossing the night sky: our cameraman, Bob Poole, captured the whole drama. Any film we made was carried daily by Arab drivers a thousand miles across the desert road to Amman, Jordan, from where it could be beamed to London. One evening, during a total blackout, I was scurrying through a hotel corridor with a bag of film for the night run to Amman and crashed through a glass door, gashing my head. I needed a few stitches and a bandage round my head for a couple of days. The Foreign Editor, John Mahoney, rang Rowena to warn her not to worry; it wasn't a war wound, I just hadn't been looking where I was going.

The conflict deteriorated into dirty, old-fashioned trench warfare between the two sides. Saddam Hussein used his chemical weapons unmercifully and tens of thousands of young Iranians died a terrible death. The Ayatollahs in Iran used martyrdom, allowing wave after wave of boy soldiers, some as young as nine, to throw themselves into minefields to pave a way for the tanks. Their promised reward…the key to Paradise. It was an enormous human tragedy taking more than a million lives from both sides and turning millions more into homeless refugees.

On top of all this, there was the increasing problem of drug addiction among the soldiers. Iran borders Afghanistan, the world's largest producer of opium. There had always been a tradition of social opium smoking in Iran but now along came the change to the stronger and cheaply available heroin.

At some point I contracted a bacterial fever and stayed in a darkened room for three days. I remember telling myself 'feed a cold, starve a fever,' as I drifted in and out of consciousness. When the fever finally abated I found myself, at the dead of night, in this grand hotel's kitchen, scrabbling around for anything resembling food.

We ended up in Basra, the country's main port, in south-eastern Iraq. The war had reached a weary stalemate but there was no end to the misleading propaganda from the military command. We decided to leave the country via the nearest exit, the long, desert road going south, a hundred miles into Kuwait.

Back in London, wealthy exiles started to arrive from Iran following the fall of the Shah. They opened fashionable restaurants and acquired some of the most expensive residential property, mostly in Kensington and Belgravia. General Fereydoun Djam, former head of the Shah's Joint Chiefs of Staff, who was living in a beautiful house on the edge of Richmond Park, invited me to lunch. Over bowls of Persian caviar we talked about the growing problem of addiction, with heroin being smuggled into London from Iran. He talked openly about his own son who had become a heroin addict, selling his expensive sports cars to fund his desperate habit. The General was on the trail of the dealer who was keeping his son supplied, aided by a couple of his friends, former members of Savak, the Shah of Iran's feared secret police. The outlook didn't look too good for that dealer! I later found out from underground contacts, which I had at that time, that he mysteriously disappeared from the drug scene, once General Djam had found him.

CHAPTER 24

A CHANGE OF LIFESTYLE

Rowena and I were married on a blazing July Saturday in 1984. The formal marriage ceremony was at Fulham Register Office and was over in a few minutes, but the main event was a different story. It began in a packed Catholic church, St. Mary of the Angels, Bayswater, where the Reverend Michael Hollings had agreed to give us a blessing, although I was Protestant and a divorcee to boot. Rowena was very happy.

One of the nuns at The Priory, Rowena's convent school in Haywards Heath, had described Father Michael as being more holy than the Pope.

Rowena on her wedding day outside the church.

Appropriately, he was also the parish priest of the Notting Hill Carnival. Our steel-band wedding reception had all the atmosphere of a street party. John Bulmer, a friend of Rowena's, generously lent us his opulent London home, the George and Dragon Hall, Notting Hill, for the reception which seemed to last the entire weekend.

Jane and John, my two children from my marriage to Gerry, were introduced to the West Indian contingent. Rowena's family had flown over from Trinidad and brought Nora with them, the wonderful black nanny who had raised Rowena in early childhood and was her mother's lifelong friend. Nora, a staunch Baptist, was stunning in her colourful dress and raised her glass high, proclaiming to all, "Praise de Lord", sending a shower of champagne everywhere. She held guests spellbound with her folklore stories told in her deep velvety voice, like treacle.

A year later Claire was born, followed by Christopher, in 1988. I took early retirement from the BBC in 1989 and a few years later, in 1993, we rented out our West London home and

148

moved to Bosham, an enchanting village on the edge of Chichester harbour, to a lovely, spacious house right on the water. Our two children had lots of fun learning to sail, how to catch fish while dreaming of one day heading off on Bosham's rising tide and crossing the ocean, maybe even all the way to Trinidad.

For a while I was happy writing articles for magazines and filling in as a presenter on World Service TV News, although I have to admit that I never felt at ease in a television studio. When I sometimes presented the news section on the Newsnight programme I never really felt part of the show. I came to believe that there wasn't really a need for a news bulletin within a current affairs programme on Channel 2. By that late hour most people were probably up to date with the routine headlines. It was Newsnight's mission to take a deeper look at the big stories of the day and hopefully to break new ground.

My decision to take early retirement was a good one for us as a family. Rowena was sixteen years my younger, but I was still only fifty-five, hopefully with plenty of time to enjoy the second half of my life. Luckily for me, the media department at Chichester College learned that I had retired to the area and invited me to introduce a 'work-related element' into their journalism course. It was fun for a short while and I'd like to think the teenage students enjoyed it.

I had no qualifications as a teacher, so it took me hours to devise interesting lessons which would often involve taking students out of college into the town to cover a real story or a current local issue. Each lesson had an end product, a written or recorded story with photographs or graphics, which could then be assessed. Some of the professional teachers advised that I should not be taking students out of college grounds without accident insurance. I thought this rather far-fetched and the students didn't care. They were really enjoying themselves.

They came to me one day with an interview they had done with an exorcist Magda Larkum, who lived just outside Chichester, asking how it could be improved. I told them that as an interview designed for radio it lacked life and colour; there was nothing in it to feed the imagination, so they should contact Magda and ask her if they could record her next exorcism. She agreed.

It was a bright sunny day when we met Magda and a friend of

hers at the former home of Sir Arthur Conan Doyle in Hindhead. The creator of Sherlock Holmes had lived for many years in this gaunt, Victorian house set back off the main road in a hollow near the Devil's Punch Bowl. The new owners, who were hoping to convert the place into a country hotel, said it was haunted. They couldn't stand the sound of screaming resounding down the corridors at night any longer, so they had sent for Magda.

I suggested that the students keep their tape recorder running from the moment we set foot in the place. Despite the sunshine outside there was an immediate chill within, our footsteps echoing off the wooden floors. The sound of creaking doors opening and a wind whining from somewhere deep inside really set the scene for a good radio story. Magda came to a standstill in one particular room,

'Undershaw' in Hindhead, designed for himself by Sir Arthur Conan Doyle.

along with her friend, who was also a medium. Magda produced a pendulum from her pocket saying, 'some unhappy spirit is trapped in here...she is a girl...she wants to re-join her mother who has long gone.' The pendulum swung gently.

Magda, a tiny woman with an ashen face, continued to make contact. 'What is your name...?' From the lips of the medium there suddenly came the voice of a fearful little girl:

'My name is Dolly...who are you?'

'My name is Magda...I am going to free you Dolly. Don't worry any more. You are going to leave here now to be with your mother again.'

'My mother...where is she?' said the girl's voice through the partly open mouth of the medium.

'She is waiting for you...go now Dolly...you are free.'

As a radio story this one was going to work. It had all the right sounds without having to add anything. We edited in the frightening experiences of those owners, who just couldn't sleep at night and I told the students that it would be perfect for a programme then running on Radio 4 called The Afternoon

Shift. We sent it to them entitled 'Ghostbusters' and they ran it exactly as it had been put together.

However there was, needless to say, a complaint from one of the teachers at Chichester College because I had taken the students out again without insurance, but it certainly gave the students a huge boost. They had got their own work on Radio 4. What could be better than that? The new owners went ahead with their plans to convert the old building into an hotel, so I assume that Magda Larkum's antics did lay the ghosts to rest.

On another occasion Chichester city centre was flooded when the River Lavant burst its banks. I set the students a very specific pictorial assignment. They were to look for a shot that somehow said to the public: whatever the calamity ... life goes on. To do that properly they were to find out what the undertakers in the city were doing with their dead.

One of them came back with a lovely picture of two undertakers standing up in a rowing boat with coffins stacked at the front. They were punting their way through the High Street, towards a church on the edge of town, where coffins were being temporarily housed ready to be taken to the crematorium. The picture made the front page of the local paper.

But, once again, the college, this time Health and Safety, raised its head. The problem was, obviously, that to buy insurance that would cover students every time they left the building would have been too costly. It made me wonder what insurances the school had taken out. Journalism and health and safety are not always easy partners. In all the years I was covering stories, sometimes in dangerous places, I was never covered by insurance. We just had an unwritten understanding that the BBC would look after our families and that was the way it worked. There is a risk in anything worthwhile.

One day a very promising student of mine, Blaize Tapp, didn't show up. I heard a teacher saying that he had phoned in and quit his course. That sounded very odd to me. I asked the teacher for more detail. He said Blaize had been having trouble at home and had decided to leave. He was calling from a railway station where there was a lot of very loud music so he couldn't be heard too well. I knew Chichester station didn't play music. I also knew that Blaize was originally from Manchester. The station he had been calling from was probably Euston where they do play music. If so, he was heading back North.

I asked his classmates to do me a favour. They were to hit the phones and find Blaize in Manchester. He was to ring me at home and reverse the charges. I wanted to make him an offer he couldn't refuse. I had spoken with his mother, who explained the family problem that had caused him to up and leave and I had told her what I planned to do.

Within a day Blaize was on the line. I told him not to quit and assured him he was going to be successful in journalism and should return to the course immediately. We had a spare bedroom at our house in Bosham and I told him he could stay with us until he got back on his feet again. He did just that. He sailed through the course with flying colours, went on to do a Diploma in journalism at Highbury College and got his first job on a newspaper. At twenty-four years of age he was on the Manchester Evening News ... the youngest news editor in the country!

Before I left the college we were granted a temporary radio licence so we could bid for a local FM slot. The students and I had great fun for five or six weeks during one summer, broadcasting news and current affairs daily to local audiences. The bid was won eventually by Spirit FM, but we gave it a good shot and a number of people, looking for a way into broadcasting, got their first chance to go on air with us. Celia Harper, for example, from Tangmere joined us with no broadcasting experience but she had a lovely voice and quite quickly got over the initial terror of being in a live studio. She went on to become a regular contributor to Spirit FM.

CHAPTER 25

THE CARIBBEAN CALLS

My wife's family, the Scotts, have been in Trinidad for two centuries, but it was still an important decision for us to leave England, to give our two young children the experience of growing up in the tropics. Rowena had retired from her job with Amnesty International and I had taken early retirement from the BBC, so there was nothing standing in our way. Claire our ten-year-old daughter and Christopher, aged just eight, were both excited about an adventure to the other side of the world, but a little nervous about fitting in to a new school.

They had enjoyed a sheltered life as small children, living on

Claire and Christopher at Bosham, West Sussex, just before we moved to live in Trinidad & Tobago.

the water's edge at Bosham. In their primary school up the road there were only white faces, blond hair and blue eyes. Now they were enrolled in a richly multi-racial Catholic prep school in the centre of Port-of-Spain, the bustling capital of Trinidad. Their aunt, Celia, had taught at St. Monica's and was able to pull a few strings.

So off we went from peaceful Bosham, nestling below the South Downs of West Sussex. We had to have a special crate made for our beautiful young Labrador, Rasta, who was to spend eight hours in the hold of the plane taking us over 4,000 miles across the Atlantic, with one stop at St. Lucia, where he was allowed off the plane for a walk. By the time we reached Trinidad's Piarco airport he was bursting. The second he was freed from his cage he charged into the pristine arrivals hall to find the nearest pillar resembling a lamp-post and let go…a golden river flooding the polished floor.

Jet black Labradors are rare in Trinidad and one of the startled floor-cleaners, who had now really got his work cut out, thought he was a leopard. 'O gawd. A dangerous animal on de loose.' Just across the water from Trinidad, in the jungles of Guyana, there are black leopards, so the specimen now emptying his bladder in the airport was given a wide berth. For Rasta, the temperature greeting him outside the airport must have been a huge shock. In Trinidad it ranges between 80°F and 100°F, with humidity to match.

The Scott family lived in Cascade, a residential area just a short walk from Port-of-Spain centre. There was a large garden with mature trees laden with fruit and huge avocados. Next to the family's bungalow stood a pretty, three-bedroomed house, built as an investment, which was now to be our home for the next five and a half years.

Rowena with her mother, Freda and father Stephen Scott.

Christopher and Claire seemed to adjust quickly to school life at St. Monica's prep school. The principal, Sister Eunan, a strict disciplinarian from Dublin, ran a tight ship with the educational standard, especially in maths, higher than it had been in sleepy Bosham. At their little school in West Sussex there had been a playground with a small vegetable garden where the pupils could grow lettuce. At St. Monica's, right in the middle of the playground, stood two thirty-foot Mango trees; the children soon learned to duck to avoid the juicy fruit when it came tumbling down.

It takes a while to get used to the sound and rhythm of life in the tropics. Daytime Port-of-Spain hums with heavy traffic, busier than on any other Caribbean island I have visited. I heard it described as 'Detroit on the tenth parallel'. After Independence in 1962, the railway lines laid by the British were abandoned along with the rolling stock, as those who could afford it preferred to travel by car. In an oil-producing country like Trinidad petrol is cheap, but now there is so much traffic that the people have to rise very early to get to work on time.

154

Many get up at dawn so as to be at their desks by nine. The rush-hour noise drones on and on and yet people on opposite sides of the road still attempt to have intimate conversations with each other. Breakfast for many is eaten on the move…a staple being 'doubles', curried chickpeas thrown in between two fried breads.

For those who live in Port-of-Spain there is one open space where townsfolk can breathe something akin to fresh air. The Queen's Park Savannah, where locals can enjoy a jog of a couple of miles around its two hundred and sixty-two acres, provides the green lungs of the city. Rasta loved it.

One of the other favourite places to take him was Maracas Bay, the nearest tropical beach to Port-of-Spain, twenty kilometres from the city, on Trinidad's lush northern coast. It's a wonderful drive offering stunning views at every turn: cathedrals of bamboo with trails down to the rain forest and far beyond to a deep turquoise sea. But you need to be careful not to get lost and be out before dark. Night descends like the drop of a stage curtain and the sound of the tropics begins. Crickets start their incessant clicks, frogs whistle and croak and if one dog even yaps a cacophonous canine orchestra echoes out all up the valley, reaching a crescendo at anything that moves in the dark.

Rasta, in the stillness of his own garden, was confused. There were movements in the bushes; animals he'd never seen before; an iguana would present its prehistoric face, a whiplash snake might hurl itself from one branch to another, a mongoose might pause in the middle of the lawn, daring him to try to catch it and the ceaseless irritation of mosquitos in their squadrons, bombarded his senses. A far cry from Bosham where a fly would be the worst he could expect. He must have asked himself whose idea it was it to bring him to Trinidad?

When the sun peeps over the hill at seven and the oven door opens onto a new day, the vibrance of colour in the gardens defies description. I was teaching myself to paint, but watercolours, at least in my hands, did not seem capable of matching reality. I switched to acrylics and slowly gained some confidence of catching nature's special tropical beauty. But perfection is elusive. Just when you think you might have got it right, the light changes and the half-completed vista is lost.

For bird watchers Trinidad is heaven. There are more than five

155

hundred different species, many of them unique. The national bird, the Scarlet Ibis, rises early in a great red cloud above the Caroni Swamp. The delicate, nectar-loving, blue hummingbird hangs in the air above a flower and is gone in a blink. The kiskidee, with its onomatopoeic name, announces its arrival for breakfast, preferably chopped banana: 'qu'est qu'il dit', it seems to be calling. It is everywhere, darting among the heliconia, poinsettia and wild orchids. You can't mistake the bird's light brown with its bright yellow front, its black beak and the white ring around its head.

Not surprisingly Trinidadians are as colourful as their environment, a rich blend of many races. The majority are of African or Indian heritage, or a mixture of the two. Then add to that mix, French-creole, Spanish, Chinese, Lebanese and Syrian blood lines, reflecting the island's history since emancipation in 1838. It is the home of calypso, soca and steel band and challenges the Rio de Janeiro street carnival as probably the most sensational street carnival in the world where, in both cases, inhibition is thrown to the winds. It starts in February the weekend before Ash Wednesday. Nine months later there's always a rise in the birth rate.

My wife's favourite part of carnival is 'jouvay,'(taken from the French 'j'ouvrai'), the opening at dawn, the last couple of hours of darkness before sun rises on Carnival Monday morning. Its ritual demands leaving home in blackness at about four in the morning and walking to the Queen's Park Savannah with friends. En route you become aware of dark shapes moving around you in a great masquerade, all heading into town, everyone dressed to kill. The excitement in the air is tangible until, at first light, music rises all over Port-of-Spain, dozens of bands leading streams of dancers swaying through the streets; you're 'jammin' with a million others, the music and the temperature hot, hot, hot, with whiffs of ganja wafting by. After three days, when the partying is finally over, Trinis take a little rest before starting to prepare for the next one. All Trinis seem to have a PhD in partying, born dancers. It's a tonic to watch them all enjoying themselves jumpin' up. My advice: don't try to compete!

Trinidadians show a great deal of tolerance to eccentrics and even to the plum crazy. In the morning rush-hour I once watched a man trying to drive an imaginary car out of a traffic jam. There is a car in front of him and one behind as he makes a right-hand signal to pull out into another lane; everyone is happy to give him plenty of room. He is driving as if he had a real steering wheel in his hands, shifting up a gear, making all the moves of a seasoned driver until he finds a spot to park, when the motorist behind slows down patiently to let him reverse. He goes into a newsagent for a paper, comes back, carefully lowers himself into an imaginary seat and tosses his rolled-up newspaper onto the back seat, which in this case was the bonnet of a car parked behind him. He turns on his engine, puts it into first gear and indicates that he's ready to pull out into the traffic again...and off he goes. I had no idea where he was finally heading or how long it would take him, but the wonderful thing was that nobody harassed him....but then he did not try to fill up with petrol!

Barbie Jardine and Grommit the vulture.

Vultures, or corbeaux, as they call them in Trinidad, are not everyone's idea of a pet. But a friend of Rowena's, Barbie Jardine, had a pet vulture she called Grommit, which she had reared from a chick after he had tumbled out of a nest.

Grommit loved Barbie and was jealous of anyone, or their pets, whom he suspected of competing with him for her affection, as Tom Mangold, an old friend from our BBC days, found out when he went to Trinidad for a few days with his new bride as part of their honeymoon. Tom, who was a well-known investigative reporter with Panorama, might be considered by some to be a bit of a tough guy, but from the moment he stepped inside Barbie's lovely house overlooking Port-of-Spain, he was on his guard. Grommit's beady eyes watched his every move.

When taking a drive into town, Barbie suggested that Tom should make a quick dash to her car. Grommit was on Tom's tail in a flash and he only just made into the passenger seat. As they set off, Grommit's massive black wings were beating on the windscreen. Barbie braked hard and the bird fell off the bonnet onto the road. She got out, gathered the bird up like a

157

pile of old bedclothes and heaved him into the bush, hoping to put him off. Grommit was not to be so easily outmanoeuvred, following them once again as they reached town with its busy traffic. He seemed to know exactly where to find the car, wherever she went. He once landed right beside us, on Carnival Monday, causing a great commotion. On another occasion Grommit arrived outside the vet's surgery. Tom might imagine that they had successfully shaken off their pursuer, when the bird soared away high and out of sight hunting for food with its spectacular telescopic vision but, as sure as night follows day, he would be waiting for Tom and his mistress when they returned.

Some evenings, with Grommit directly outside his bedroom door, Tom used to say that he slept with his eyes open. 'You haven't felt fear until you've heard the sound of a vulture's wings sweeping across the wooden floor at the dead of night.'

Grommit stayed with Barbie for fourteen years before falling in love with a real bird and flying off into the sunset. 'The story of my life,' she commented ruefully. Before he left us Grommit starred in a much-loved children's book by Barbie's brother-in-law, Andy Campbell.

Celia Scott, Rowena's sister, hosted her own music programme on Radio 97 in Trinidad and became a household name. Through her I was invited to join the station to help them develop a news and current affairs department. There is no better way to learn more about a country than becoming a local journalist. My knowledge of Trinidad was still fairly limited even though I had been there many times before, on holiday.

Now I was living in Trinidad, I had time to find out what made the place tick. The first obstacle was deciphering the way people speak English. Trinidad creole is a strange mixture of English and French and it takes some time to tune your ear to the variations of the local patois. After five years of schooling Claire and Christopher became fluent. So much so, that when they were having a conversation in local dialect, they sounded to me like completely different people.

The first series of programmes I did for the radio station was on literacy. Officially, Trinidad was ninety-seven percent literate but tutors at the teacher training college in Trinidad told me that was way off. It was nearer sixty per cent. The higher figure referred to the number of children listed as having started primary school. It did not take account of the numbers who didn't stay to learn anything.

Students, learning to be teachers in state schools, were taught standard English using local dialect so that they might better communicate with the children. I found the result quite difficult to follow, but the programmes I produced from recordings in various classrooms, seemed popular among listeners, so we decided to tackle adult literacy as well. I joined some evening classes in downtown Port-of-Spain and slowly the students got used to having me among them with a tape-recorder.

There was a man in his late fifties who was delighted that at long last he could read the first page of his favourite cowboy novel. Despite being illiterate he had been very successful in business. He was well-dressed, had a smart car and lived in a nice house. We talked at length about the secret of his success. He used to say that the key was delegation. 'I does get people to fill in any forms I need, like the application for a driver's licence and anything else with words in it to do with the Government. I does delegate someone to sit the written test for a driver's licence.'

He was charmingly frank about the way he'd made his way in life without anyone in business knowing that he couldn't read a word. Delegation at every turn, he said, was the way he kept his secret. Finally I asked him to tell me about the business he had so painstakingly built up? He said, 'I is a printer.' He could see I was amazed.

'Delegation, David. Delegation.'

A touch of Trinidad magic happened one Christmas when John Huson, my oldest friend from National Service days, came to visit us. Normally, at this time of year, the weather is perfect in the Caribbean but from the moment he landed it rained ceaselessly and he quickly became the subject of local gossip. They called him Rainman and wanted to know more about him and his itinerary while on holiday so they could avoid getting caught in the rain. In no time the gossips knew exactly what John looked like: short, plump at the time, bald as a coot; that he came from Nottinghamshire, was a lifetime supporter of Nottingham Forest football club and during a weekend trip we made to Tobago someone had stolen his very expensive new trainers. They also knew that with a bit of persistent detective work and police help he had traced the thief back to his village

159

in the hills and, amazingly, the stolen trainers had been handed back to him. No-one had wanted to upset Rainman.

I tell you all this because one day, back in Trinidad, John and I stopped at the Look-out point above Maracas Bay to take in the spectacular view. It is a favourite spot for day-trippers with cameras, and most importantly for experienced calypsonians to ply their trade. They will enrapture someone and sing a story about them, often with intimate detail. Uncannily the calypsonian who strummed a tune for John didn't leave much out of his story:

"Word creepin' round de island bout dis white man called Rainman. Wherever he does go Heaven does open up and wash out de place. Right now supposed to be dry season, wid a lot a sun, but since Rainman arrive it does be comin' down in swords.

'Rainman' John Huson, my oldest living friend from National Service days, manning the barbecue. Here he is a slim version of what he used to be.

"Everyone talkin' bout dis man and askin' how we go spot de Rainman when we see him passin'.

"De story is dat he ghost-white, bald like a bishop; wearing a pair a blue shorts – moving through de bush on two lil' short white legs, quick,

quick, like chicken in a hurry. News is dat he go be passin' through de place dis Sunday near de parishes of Carapichaima and Rampanalgas, between dawn an' breakfast, on big white horse given to him by de Sheriff of Nottingham and Maid Moron.

"In Tobago poor Rainman was robbed of he magic shoes he bought in South Africa and in de night drumbeat spread word dat Rainman vex and he comin' for dem shoes. Sleepin' police even wake up to help hunt for de tief. Rainman climb in he leaf-green jeep and wake up de parrots wid he fast drivin' over de bush trail. De magic spell on dem shoes guide Rainman to de right place. De villagers are frightened when dey realise it is Rainman who get robbed.' Oh Gawd' de people bawl.

Supposin' he make de sun disappear again an' black clouds mash-up de water spouts.' Nobody want to take dat chance. Detective Rainman fix he eagle eye on dem … and from dis place an dat come people carryin' dem magic shoes. Rainman smile. De police smile. Even de tief smile dat Rainman happy and dat de sun go smile too.

"Rainman wake up early on he final day … beachcombin' among de bare bumsies on Maracas Bay and bravin' de fallin' coconuts. Everyone wanted Rainman to stay now and not return to de land of icicles an' Nottingham Forest. He promise to come back but say he must go. Nottingham Forest need him. De Old Coach House need him too, to knock back de pints stretchin' across de bar for de safe return of their intrepid adventurer. As flight BW 900 reach fuh de sky de steelband music start to carry a song on de wind. 'Dey seek him here, dey seek him there, dey seek dat Rainman everywhere. Gawd bless Rainman."

CHAPTER 26

THE HAUNTED ISLAND

Local fishermen are still reluctant to set foot on its shoreline for fear of being taken by the spirits, who they believe to haunt the place. These days it's mostly foreign yachtsmen who find their way to Chacachacare and anchor, just as Columbus did in 1498, among the bottle-nosed dolphins and hawksbill turtles in Marine Bay. Not a soul lives on the island anymore and there is nothing to hint at events that took place down the ages, except for a few vandalised buildings almost overtaken by dense forest.

There is nobody to explain that this little island, Trinidad and Tobago's farthest out-post, only six miles from Venezuela's Paria penin-sula, was at one time a springboard for the revol-ution that finally ended Spanish control of South America. Later, it was also the last sanctuary for society's outcasts, held there in a leper colony.

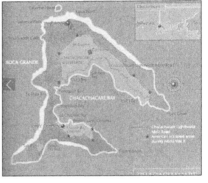

The island of Chacachacare, Trinidad's farthest outpost, now abandoned.

It is not just superstition that keeps many local people away. To reach Chacachacare you need to set out from Port-of-Spain. It takes half-an-hour by motor boat. There are no amenities, no electricity, so you must take everything, food and water, but it is a magical spot, blissfully peaceful, with the perfume of wild orchids on the breeze and forty types of flora and fauna not found anywhere else in Trinidad and Tobago. After dark, any serious movement in the bush is likely to be from red squirrels thriving among the mango trees where the lepers were buried long ago, or it might be the crack and crunch of giant iguanas looking for their supper. From the old lighthouse, with its breath-taking sunset view over the Caribbean, the waves can be seen breaking on the Venezuelan shore. Close your eyes as you stand among the broken timbers of the old convent and Chacachacare will whisper its story, a tale of enormous courage among French Dominican nursing sisters who risked their lives coming here to care for the lepers.

My companions on this trip are photographer Catherine Gillo, an old school friend of Rowena and Sister Marie Therese Retout of the same French Dominican Order, who became their archivist after uncovering their story in 1993.

Sister Marie Therese Retout.

Hidden away in an old storeroom at Holy Name Convent in Port-of-Spain she found cobwebbed boxes riddled with termites. Inside were the diaries of the sisters who served on Chacachacare, all written in French. Sr. Marie Therese made English translations: heart-rending descriptions of their determination to keep fighting a hideous disease for which there was no cure until the middle of the twentieth century. It was the spiritual strength of these good sisters, all from Bonnay in the Burgundy region of France, that bound them together in their isolation from the rest of the world. The government of the day built places for everyone to live and a house for a resident doctor. Drinking water, food and medical supplies were all brought in by boat. Beyond that it was candles and courage.

The original Dominican sisters of St. Catherine of Siena had left France for Trinidad in 1868, at the invitation of the colonial government which was, in reality, more of a desperate plea for help in running a leprosarium which had been established at Cocorite, near the capital, in 1845. Leprosy had been brought to Trinidad on a tide of East Indian immigration, recruited to fill the serious labour shortage that followed the end of slavery. The sisters fought a losing battle at Cocorite because so many patients would register for treatment at the medical centre but then abscond, spreading the disease at such an alarming rate through Port-of-Spain that the government was forced to take drastic action. Normal life in the city was being seriously threatened and the isolation of the lepers was seen as imperative. The remoteness of Chacachacare came to their attention: the few people living there were given eviction orders and to offset the cost of building a leprosarium on the island income tax was introduced for the first time. There was a public outcry, but there were no better options. To avoid hysteria among the population and to protect the lepers, the time and date of the first transfer of patients was a state secret. A nun's diary for 10th May 1922 recalls the occasion:

"At six in the morning, the patients were seized with horror when news spread throughout the wards that the whole place was surrounded and cordoned off by policemen on foot and on horseback. A dead silence reigned, as it was impossible to escape. All had to be resigned to their fate. Some were sobbing and at the sight of such evident distress in the poor sufferers, even the policemen were moved with compassion. A crowd of onlookers gathered outside to see the patients being escorted by policemen to the Cocorite pier where a steamer was waiting to take them to Chacachacare."

The new settlement on Chacachacare had a hospital, a common refectory, a bakery, kitchens, store rooms and cottages for patients… on Coco Bay for men and on Sanders Bay for women. By 1926 a convent, on a hill overlooking Marine Bay, had been built for the sisters. Standing in the middle of what's left of it, as the forest takes over, I can easily visualise figures in black and white trekking through the waning evening light to vespers. For all of them the physical effort of trying to keep the disease at bay was enormous. Patients, especially those whose limbs had become badly deformed and infected, went through periods of terrible agony. Their wailing could be heard in the night. One of the sisters had put in so much effort to ease their pain that on the last lap up the hill to the convent, where she was going to rest, she had a heart attack and died.

Two of the ten sisters buried in the little cemetery near the convent at Marine Bay, died of leprosy. One of them, Sr. Rose de Saint Marie Vebert, originally from Paris, had suffered with the disease for eighteen years while she lived among the patients at Sanders. The leprosy had taken away her sight and had hideously distorted her once attractive face. Her tongue was so swollen she could barely speak. The sisters sang hymns and canticles by her bedside to help her regain her calm when terrible fits shook her body. Finally she breathed her last and the sisters carried her body to the chapel. While she lay there something extraordinary happened: all traces of the awful disease which had twisted her face slowly disappeared and she looked like her former self, quite beautiful, as though she was simply enjoying a sleep.

Throughout the second world war, Chacachacare remained in isolation, although German U-boats regularly patrolled in the Gulf of Paria threatening Atlantic shipping. The waters around Trinidad are littered with wrecks: occasionally the sisters would wake to see a U-boat surfaced offshore, flying the swastika, but no Germans ever set foot on the island.

The fight for survival in the loneliness of the leper colony continued long after the rest of the world was finally able to lick its wounds in recovery. With the end of the war a combination of new drugs was produced to treat leprosy successfully, but the application by intravenous injection was slow and extremely painful. Each patient had to be given several injections a day. One nursing sister wrote in her diary for December 31, 1945 that throughout the year she alone had given 10,620 injections to 388 patients including 38 children.

The Second World War also took its toll on recruitment to the religious life. There were no replacements in prospect for the ageing Dominican sisters, so their gradual withdrawal from Chacachacare began. Local volunteer nurses were trained to care for the lepers, but it was a big culture shock for them, cut off from family and friends. They found it very difficult to adjust to such a relentlessly tough, simple, life with few comforts. With the success of new treatments the colony was finally closed on July 23, 1984 and the island left to rest. The Dominican sisters had given eighty-two years of continuous service to their cause.

Chacachacare's significance however, in the swashbuckling history of Trinidad and Tobago, began much earlier than the leper colony. Five hundred years ago, Amerindians on the island watched Columbus sail his fleet through the rocky waterway, the Dragon's Mouth, which separates the island from Venezuela. There is still an overgrown track leading through the forest from La Tinta Bay to the ruins of a house where, in 1813, an English-trained Trinidadian soldier, Santiago Moreno, secretly plotted to help Simon Bolivar defeat the Conquistadores in the South American Wars of Independence.

Officially Spain and England were at peace. The British governor in Port-of-Spain had no idea that a private army was being prepared in his territory for battle. In South America, at that time, there were thousands of men in hiding from the Spaniards, waiting for a liberator behind whom they could rally. The man they hoped would one day lead the revolution, Simon Bolivar, was in exile in Jamaica.

For years Santiago Moreno's preparations on Chacachacare went on unnoticed by outsiders. Then, somehow, the Spaniards got suspicious of the military activity across the water and sent a letter of protest to the English Governor of Trinidad and Tobago. The letter was intercepted by supporters of Moreno, in Port-of-Spain, who kept it hidden for days until Moreno signalled that he was ready to attack the Spaniards.

At three o'clock in the morning, with a force of forty-five experienced Trinidadian soldiers, Moreno invaded a Spanish fort at Guiria just across the Dragon's Mouth. Though Moreno's men were heavily outnumbered they had the element of surprise and were overwhelming the defences before the Spaniards even woke up. It was a rout and word spread quickly of a big defeat for the Conquistadores. It bolstered the courage of those in hiding and they came to join Moreno's army, until its fighting strength was soon five thousand strong and counting, as they moved westward to attack other Spanish garrisons.

In that first year, the Spaniards were slow to take the threat seriously; they had enjoyed such a stranglehold over South America for so long it was hard for them to imagine ever losing control. Simon Bolivar, from his exile in Jamaica, had tried hard to awaken British interest in the reign of terror being inflicted on the South American people in the name of the Spanish monarchy. He was heartened by the success of Santiago Moreno's growing army and came out of exile to lead all those ready to lay down their lives for freedom from Spain. The forces allied to the revolution were soon to be swelled by English and Irish soldiers, wearing the uniforms that had seen them through the Battle of Waterloo, now swearing allegiance to Bolivar. They endured great hardship in the jungles and the freezing highlands of Venezuela in winter. Four of the original group of Trinidadians that left Chacachacare with Moreno had now risen to be generals leading their own units.

The British Admiral, Thomas Cochrane, the tenth Earl of Dundonald, a man with a Quixotic sense of adventure, took leave of absence from the Royal Navy to join Bolivar's cause, leading a mercenary fleet against the Spanish and the Portuguese. Their joint effort, when combined with Bolivar's land forces, eventually came together to win a decisive victory over at the Battle of Carabobo, to the west of Caracas, in 1821. Santiago Moreno returned to Chacachacare, where he and his wife were later given a hero's welcome in Port-of-Spain. Nobody breathed a word about the early warning letter from the Spaniards, which may have eventually arrived on the governor's desk, too late for him to do anything about it.

CHAPTER 27

SOLDIERS FROM THE SUN

There are more than thirty commercial radio stations in Trinidad and Tobago, all chasing a slice of the same market with a population of only 1.4 million, so competition is fierce. The station I worked for, on top of the Long Circular Mall in Trinidad, decided to introduce something more intellectually stimulating with Radio 104, which would provide a diet of news, current affairs features, jazz and classical music, which to me seemed to be a formula that might find favour with several age groups. It was the kind of radio with which I was most at ease and I looked forward to helping a few budding journalists enjoy the experience. The BBC in London was happy to help by giving us free access to a wide range of classical records, while the news department generously gave permission for us to re-write and use any stories from BBC correspondents around the world, provided we attributed the source.

My idea of interesting radio was never going to be what the majority of listeners in Trinidad might want to hear. In Britain, Radio 4 news attracts the largest audience with more than ten million listeners, with fifty-six being the average age of those tuning in. Radio audiences in Trinidad and Tobago are much younger and their preferences are not centred on global news. Quite rightly, they are interested in what's happening on their own doorstep and want programmes that reflect their own unique culture. Radio 104 was offering an alternative away from the Americanisation of the local air waves, on which local advertisers battered listeners' ear drums day and night. For a start I devised a programme called 'Soldiers from the Sun,' which would explore the Caribbean's rich history of war through the ages, from 1939-45 right back to the 1600s and Blackbeard the Pirate.

More than 30,000 Trinidadians and other West Indians fought alongside the British forces in World War II. There were Trinidadians who served with distinction in RAF Bomber Command on countless raids over Germany, among them Ulric Cross, DSO DFC a navigator on bombing missions who went on to become a High Court judge in Trinidad.

For these programmes I used Gaylord Kelshall, curator of Trinidad's Military Museum and himself an authority on the U-Boat War in the Atlantic, to guide us through the pivotal role Trinidad played in the supply chain for the forces in Europe, providing both newly-trained American reinforcements and fuel oil, both of which became even more important when America joined the war in 1941, following the Japanese destruction of Pearl Harbour. Trinidad's oil refinery at Point-a-Pierre provided a vital strategic facility in the Gulf Paria.

A series of radio programmes – Soldiers from the Sun – which I made in Trinidad about West Indians at war down the ages – won a major award but was never transmitted because the radio station boss wasn't interested in pre-independence history.

The race was now on to get radar up and running in the fight against German U-boats. John Logie Baird, the Scottish inventor of television, who had been secretly working on the development of radar since the 1920s, was dispatched to Trinidad to come up with a solution to the U-boat threat as fast as possible. His radar gave the Royal Navy and the Air Force eyes over the waves, which together with the introduction of the newly invented Asdic for sounding the depth of the ocean from the ships, gradually changed the outlook in the battle of the Atlantic.

New calypsos were performed, inspired by the economic importance of the Americans in local life: Trinidad's famous calypsonian, the 'Mighty Sparrow', came up with a new tune 'round de corner posin…bet yuh life it sometin' deh sellin.'

The second programme followed Trinidadians in the British West Indies Regiment during the World War I, describing their involvement in the Battle of the Somme. In 1916 one of my wife's relatives, Captain Stuart Scott, a son of the Mayor of Port-of-Spain, Frederick E. Scott, was wounded in the first half hour of the Battle of La Boiselle. He lay all day in no man's land with machine gun bullets in his hip, before managing to crawl back to his own lines. After the war Stuart built a house in Trinidad and named it after that battle. The village of La Boiselle slowly grew up around Stuart's house, though not many of the people who now live there are aware of its origin.

Subsequent programmes, covering the development in Trinidad of a West Indies militia in the 1800s under General Thomas Picton, detailed battles in West Africa against the slavers. We broadcast programmes on what life had been like in Trinidad during those dangerous, swashbuckling days, when British officers often settled their differences with swords or pistol duals on the Savannah in the centre of Port-of-Spain. The duelling tradition even spread to competing merchants in the city and among head servants on the plantations. Though some people would prefer them to be scrapped there are still street names all over Port-of-Spain linking it to its illustrious colonial history: Abercromby, Buller, Waterloo, Kitchener, Trafalgar … and so on.

In the final programme we described the Spanish-Amerindian wars and the hostile reception Columbus received when he landed in Trinidad in 1498. He was looking for gold. But the Arawak and Carib tribes, cannibalistic at the time, saw something new to eat and slew the white invading soldiers with a rain of arrows.

The scourge of the Spaniards, who later took Trinidad, was the infamous Blackbeard the pirate, Edward Teach, a Bristol-born merchantman in the reign of Queen Anne, who turned privateer in the early 1700s, flying the skull and crossbones over his ship.

These six programmes were each originally designed to be half an hour long, but the local boss of the radio station at the time thought this was too long a span to retain his listeners' attention, so we edited them down to ten minutes. He then took the decision not to transmit them at all, because he ruled that there was no appetite for pre-independence history. The tapes gathered dust on a shelf in his office for a year. When the Caribbean Media Awards ceremony was held in Trinidad, the organisers asked for submissions from local radio stations. Someone suggested entering 'Soldiers from the Sun.' It won! Even though the radio station collected the award, the programmes were still not transmitted and probably never have been: back on the shelf gathering more dust.

CHAPTER 28

WAITING FOR THE BOMB SQUAD

It is just after lunch in the Long Circular Mall and the place is packed, when we get word in the radio station that there is a bomb about to go off in one of the shops downstairs. This is most unusual: Trinidad doesn't have bomb scares. It has plenty of murders and kidnappings, but this is the first bomb scare. The police have been informed and they have told the army who in turn say they are now trying to locate the bomb squad. Nobody is aware that Trinidad has such an elite unit as a bomb squad. The locals are well used to fire drills in the Mall so, this time, when the alarms start blaring there is a calm, unhurried evacuation from the building and half-an-hour later the place is empty. Several hundred people are now assembled in the car park waiting for a big bang. Trinidadians love high drama and no-one wants to miss the action.

By 3pm the numbers in the car park have swelled...word has spread that the Mall is the place to be. More ice-cream sellers have arrived and a little lady is selling her home-made chicken roti. They have no conception of the carnage a bomb can wreak, except from what they've seen in movies. Trinidad is not Beirut. Everyone is interested to see what Trinidad's very own bomb squad looks like in action. There's a feeling of pride in the idea that such a specialist organisation even exists.

At 4pm there is still no sign of them. Not a whisper. They've had enough time to select and train a bomb squad, or maybe they've all gone fishing and it's taking time to reel them in. Among the crowd, boredom is beginning to show itself and some are a little annoyed that it's taking so much time. I am in the car park with Raymond, one of our trainee broadcasters, so I tell him it's time for us to start planning our story. It's an otherwise quiet news day and whichever way the story ends we are going back into the building soon to prepare our 6pm bulletin. I reassure Raymond that if the bomb, or whatever it is, was going to explode it would have done so by now. To be honest it was looking more like a hoax.

Just after 5pm the 'Trinidad Bomb Squad' actually arrives, or rather he arrives, one enormous barn-door of a man in camouflage, reflector sunglasses and bling, a revolver slung low on his hip. He is Mr T. from the 'A' Team. There is no-one else with him and he carries no specialist equipment, though he is dressed to kill. Raymond wants to know what we are going to ask our superhero. Having already written the story so far, in my head, I tell him there is only one question…'What kept you? People here have been waiting for more than three hours.' Raymond is a big man himself and marches up to Superman to deliver the question. The man is immediately indignant.

'I am very busy. I have a lotta things to attend to before coming here.' He makes it sound as though he's spent the afternoon defusing bombs all over Trinidad and rambles on about the pressure of work on his precious time and how it's all a matter of priorities. It's hilarious. An exasperated security official from the Mall interrupts, asking him if he could now spare some of his precious time to actually have a look at the bomb before it blows us all to smithereens. Superman marches off at the double to where an abandoned hold-all, with suspicious-looking electronic equipment inside, lays behind a shop door.

Our hero is a little short on finesse. He holds the bag up to his ear and rips it wide open. Some of the bits fall on the floor. There is absolute silence. Then comes the pronouncement of the Bomb Squad: 'It harmless. Allyuh, can all go home,' and he's off to another assignment in his busy day.

There is a ripple of disappointment through some of the crowd that Trinidad's first bomb scare turned out to be such a damp squib, but, for us, it made an amusing tale on the 6pm news.

CHAPTER 29

BLANCHISSEUSE

Every day in Trinidad and Tobago is an adventure for our family as we discover something new, which I'm sure was why Rowena wanted our children to enjoy the experience of growing up in the tropics. Five hundred years of pre-Independence history in which people of so many nationalities have settled and intermarried, make it the multi-racial melting pot it is today. No wonder the locals are known as the Rainbow People.

Early Sunday morning we are up and on our way, with Rasta, to Blanchisseuse on the northern coast. By 8am we are on the beach with a fire going to cook bacon and eggs for breakfast and are joined by friends, Miranda and Seamus Bell from South Africa. We have sweet mango from the garden and strong Colombian coffee. Rasta has headed for a small lagoon where a mountain river flows into the sea and looks as though he too has found paradise. In the shallows he disturbs a shoal of tadpoles with heads the size of a sixpence which will turn into very large frogs, eager to give us a deep-throated nightly recital as dark descends.

Rowena has developed a close friendship with Miranda. They are both caring, outgoing people with a love of life and her two children, Rosie and Chris are about the same age as Claire and Christopher. They build a fleet of sturdy little boats out of coconut leaves and shells, complete with rudders and sails... a skill our two children learned from Christopher Crocker, an intrepid sailor, who has known Rowena since their childhood days in Trinidad. I remember watching him patiently showing the children how to build these little vessels which sailed so well. A group of youngsters from the village were fascinated too; much to my surprise they had never seen it done before and were really keen to learn.

In the late afternoon as the searing heat cools a little, the first of the red crabs pops out of a hole in the sand; I watch it approach an abandoned cigarette packet and crush it in two with an outsize claw. Their much bigger brothers will be out after

174

dark and they can rip their way out of a sack in seconds. Rowena sits on a rock with Claire looking out to sea and tells her that there is nothing between us right here and Africa.

Above the beach, up a steep pathway through the palm trees, sits the spacious, L-shaped hacienda built on family land by Rowena's cousin, Ronald Harford. The Spanish style is modelled on a house of Ronald's friend who has his villa in the Amazon basin of Venezuela. Its vast patio with swimming pool

Freda Scott and her daughter Rowena enjoying a dip in the pool at Ronald Harford's hacienda.

is at the same level as the swaying palms and their coco-nuts, but from the only road leading to Blanchisseuse you would never know such a place existed. I imagine it as the perfect hideaway for a south American drug baron, sturdily built, well protected and easily defended on its hilltop. Ronald, a very successful banker, is so generous, letting members of the Scott family stay there whenever. It is a peaceful ret-reat from the hectic hustle of Port-of-Spain, a perfect spot to

paint, enclosed by a hundred shades of green. At night, above the sounds of the pitch-black forest, the cicadas and frogs, there is only the comforting, distant crash of the waves below.

Rowena and I had been coming to the Caribbean for holidays long before we decided to try living there. Claire was only two months old when we first took her to the beautiful island of Grenada, her grandmother's birthplace. Old wives' tales abound in these islands: before Rowena knew she was pregnant a horse-whip snake flung itself from a tree onto her shoulders as we were taking an evening stroll. Apparently it's a sign that a baby is on its way. Sure enough a couple of days later, when she had a medical check, she discovered it was true. Rowena was eight weeks pregnant.

Both Claire and Rowena have always been great sleepers. Minutes after their heads touch the pillow they are gone. I have always envied that ability because I am just the opposite, sometimes tossing and turning for hours. Claire slept so peacefully in her Moses basket, either hanging from the ceiling inside a mosquito net or slung from the branch of an almond tree on the beach. Christopher, like me, is a poor sleeper. But both of them share a love of Afro-Caribbean music and like their mother knows how to move fluidly to its beat. Christopher was a toddler, still in nappies, when he first swayed to the sound of reggae pounding from massive speakers on the beach at Pigeon Point, Tobago. Decades later, as a DJ, he still has the same passion for top-quality sound. His bedroom is virtually a recording studio.

During my marriage to Gerry, I got the hang of how to do the foxtrot. With Rowena I learned how to move to the music of the Caribbean. In fact almost everything I know about the tropics came from her and her family and the wonderful friends we made. My experiences as a journalist in the Caribbean were the icing on the cake. For my children, in particular, these are special memories that will stay with them forever: chugging downriver in the Caroni Swamp and seeing their first alligator, a cayman, edging alongside the boat and then, suddenly directly above them a boa constrictor curled threatening to strike.

CHAPTER 30

SPICE ISLAND

The fount of all knowledge about my wife's family history was Rowena's mother Freda. She seemed to know everyone and was treated like a celebrity whenever she returned to her birthplace Grenada, where her side of the family, the Harfords, had lived on plantations for several hundred years. The earliest records show that their descendants, through marriage into the De Bellot family, first came to Grenada with General Abercromby's army in 1796.

My first experience of life in Grenada's superb countryside was at Vendome, a family estate five miles north of the capital St. George's, where the road winds its way up into the cool of the rainforest. There is more rainfall up there and anything grows.

Grenada has been described as an emerald in a sea of sapphire and so it is, the most southerly of the Windward Islands, 90 miles north of Trinidad and Tobago, where the pace of life is slow and easy. The north-east trade winds from the Atlantic keep the island refreshingly cool for most of the year, although the daytime temperature ranges from 85 degrees Fahrenheit to 95 degrees in the hot months of August to November. On an early evening stroll through the plantation at Vendome the fragrance of some of the many spices, cinnamon, cloves, ginger and most importantly nutmeg, the country's main export crop along with bananas, is everywhere.

The old plantation house, with its Demerara windows wide open to catch the breeze, overlooks acres of coconut palms and cocoa with a view down to the Caribbean sea in the distance. In the bush there are the graves of early family descendants. Freda and Rowena loved to recount the family history to which I have listened for hours, enthralled while imagining that I could feel the presence of those ghosts from the past, coming alive with their vivid storytelling. Outside, the cocoa drying trays are still to be found, where the bare feet of slaves had once sorted the young pods.

Grenada was first colonised by the French in the mid-17th

century and so many of the place names in the island are from that period: L'Esterre and Baccolet were two of the family estates they talked about, from whence daughters would be sent to school in England, returning in early womanhood in the hope of finding suitable husbands.

Rowena's mother has a story she has kept quiet for many decades. Before she met and married Stephen Scott in Trinidad, she had a secret lover in Grenada. He was black and in those

Freda, the matriarch of the Scott family and fount of all knowledge on their Caribbean history over the last two hundred years.

days such relationships were forbidden among women in white society, but Freda was in love and went to great lengths to protect her clandestine affair. Her lover was from a good Grenadian family but he had a reputation as a womaniser and in the end she decided that if she eloped with him, she would be the one to be hurt, so she married Stephen, a devout Catholic and kept her secret throughout their lives together. Before Freda died at the grand old age of 98 she gave Rowena the ring her lover had once put on her finger. She had kept it well hidden all those years.

Rowena and I were shown a rare photograph, perhaps the only one in existence, of her mother and her lover standing by a sports car outside Mount Valentine, a beautifully proportioned plantation house once owned by her aunt, Pearl, overlooking the deep-water harbour of St. George's and the Carenage. The new owner, Diane Yohannen from London, had superbly refurbished the old place and she found the framed photograph left behind in a corner of the drawing room, though she knew nothing of its secrets. Over tea, Rowena told her the story. Diane kindly commissioned me to paint the stunning view of St. George's from her garden.

To spend an evening with Rowena and her mother at

Vendome was like a local history lesson, especially when her sister Rosamund was alive. At the outset of the second world war, Rosamund, who had married an English Royal Navy officer, was on her way to join him in England. It was September 1939 and Rosamund was in the early stages of pregnancy. She had managed to get one of the passenger berths aboard the British oil tanker the Regent Tiger. At this time Britain did not possess the means of eliminating the German U-Boat threat and their wolf packs were marauding merchant shipping in the Atlantic and North Sea. It was an extremely necessary but dangerous journey for any merchant ship.

All went well for the Regent Tiger until she was approaching the Bay of Biscay. Lt. Kommander Gerhard Glattes, aboard U-39, a Type 1XA submarine, brought the tanker into his periscope sights and closed in. It was part of his mission to stop Allied food and oil supplies reaching Europe. Honourably he signalled the Regent Tiger giving them twenty minutes to abandon ship.

Rosamund and other passengers had no time to collect any of their belongings. 'We just went into the sea with just the clothes we were wearing, nothing else,' she said.

When the last of the crew had left their ship, Kommander Glattes released his torpedoes. The Regent Tiger was an easy target and sank within minutes. Rosamund and the others were in the water for only a few hours before being rescued by another British cargo ship and eventually brought to England. She came ashore bedraggled and penniless and found her way to the Army and Navy Club in London, seeking help. Tragically her husband was killed, in action at sea, before he had a chance to see his son, George.

When the war was over Rosamund returned to Grenada with George aboard a cruise ship. She was a handsome woman and the German captain of the ship invited her to dine with him at his table. Not surprisingly Rosamund turned him down, saying she was busy. 'I did not like Germans and there was something about the captain that made me wary,' she later said.

The captain persisted, but each time he was rejected. Finally he asked her why she disliked Germans so much and reluctantly she told him what had happened in September 1939 to the Regent Tiger. He then told her that his name was Gerhard Glattes and that by amazing coincidence he had been the commander of U-39 at the time; it was he who sank the ship. The day after he had sunk the tanker his submarine was intercepted by a British frigate and he and his crew had been taken prisoner. Rosamund never did take up his offer of dinner and the captain left her alone.

Safely back in Grenada she spent the rest of her life quietly at Vendome with her son managing the estate, but unfortunately he let the old house slip into awful disrepair and when Hurricane Ivan struck Grenada in 2004 it collapsed. George was able to shelter in a stone cellar for two days and emerged to a pile of rubble. The Harford family generously built him a bungalow on the same spot to see out his days. That hurricane devastated Grenada, leaving so very many people homeless and felling most of its valuable nutmeg trees, which took years to replace.

In a book called The Guava Tree about the Harford family at Vendome, Rowena wrote an evocative foreword recalling her idyllic childhood holidays on the estate: 'My tree. I race down the gap as fast as my legs can carry me, the soft red earth squeezing through my toes as I run, stop, and look up into the branches. Grandpa has just agreed to let me have it. And of all the hundreds of trees on the plantation this one was the one I'd chosen and he'd given it to me. I could have had a nutmeg tree, a clove or even cinnamon tree but the young Guava tree was the one I wanted. Now it's mine. Triumphantly I stroke the smooth bark and let my fingers trace the lines up to the lowest branch, hold tight, then pull myself up to sit in the fork, my bare legs dangling. I lean against the trunk and survey my domain: the surrounding hills, the pasture, the huge volcanic rocks belched up centuries ago, the curve of the gap sweeping down to the village below and across the road, the village school.

'In the early morning I liked nothing better than to collect the brown and white eggs from the chicken coop, where, in the straw-filled nesting boxes, a wooden egg or two nestled to encourage the hens to lay. Grandpa would write the date on the eggs laid that day and they were stored in a wooden rack to be used in order. Deep saffron yolks I never tasted again until many years later at the house of a friend, in Colombia.

If Grandpa needed to drive into town I'd help him crank his black Ford, registration number P19 ... and that was how he was known in the island, Number Nineteen. The villagers would scatter when they heard his car coming up the hill past Anandale and Snug Corner and Beaulieu, hooting at every corner.'

Rowena and I met an old man in town who remembered her Grandpa vividly, reminding her that he was also known as Second Gear because he never learned to get beyond that.

Nicknames are very widely used in Grenada and when they read the latest death notices on radio every morning, as they do, they go on and on and on and the presenter sometimes gives a great sigh in between each one. 'Such-and-such a person, also known as Red or Copper, sometimes known as Jumpy or Bumps (big sigh) has passed away at his home in....'

Grenada and its people have a natural charm and it's hard to imagine the island tearing itself apart over politics, although it was on the brink of civil war when Rowena and I were there in the early 1980s when Maurice Bishop was the Prime Minister. He was a charismatic figure and I met him several times at press conferences where he came across as a democratic socialist. He seemed to be close to Castro and was using Cuban money and technical skills to help improve Grenada's infrastructure, at least that is what he said. Rowena had gone through what she called her 'Marxist period' in Colombia in the slipstream of Che Guevara's popularity and thought Maurice Bishop would be good for Grenada.

We hadn't realised that a hard-line Communist faction within Bishop's government and in his political party, the New Jewel Movement, was gaining more and more influence over the direction the country was taking. His own Deputy Prime Minister, Bernard Coard, who led that rebel faction, staged a coup on October 19, 1983, in which Bishop and several of his associates were brutally murdered. It sent shock waves through the Caribbean...and Washington. The White House had been worried for some time about Soviet-Cuban involvement in Grenada which commands a strategic position in the Caribbean. With Bishop dead, and Grenada up for grabs, every power-hungry adventurer in the islands might decide he was a Marxist and get big ideas. That seems to have been the White House thinking. The diplomats were especially concerned that Soviet-Cuban money had helped build a new airport at Point Salines, nearer the capital, which had a runway large enough to cope with heavy military aircraft: Soviet and Cuban bombers for example.

The old airfield, Pearls Airport, was tiny and situated in the island's north east near Grenville, a long, bumpy drive to the capital. The Grenadians had been thinking about building a new, more convenient airport for decades but had put it off because the island's tourist industry was too small to support the enormous cost involved. When Bishop's New Jewel Movement took power they expressed the thought that a new airport might even be a means of capitalist infiltration and exploitation, but Bishop changed his mind and persuaded the Cubans to take the lead on the airport project, leaving the Grenadians to raise about half the cost.

The U.S refused to aid the project, convinced that the new regime in Grenada cared more about the political and military benefits of a large new airport than about improving the tourist industry. They also sabotaged the chances of any Western European funding for the airport, which only added to the list of grievances against the United States.

It took a while for the US to make its case for intervention in Grenada. Soviet trade officials had said they were trying to give Grenada support but did not want to become embroiled in a confrontation with America. However it subsequently came to light that a secret arms agreement between the USSR and Grenada, signed in Havana in 1980, provided arms and ammunition over a period of a year. It included mortars, machine guns, grenade launchers, support equipment and spare parts. The Soviets also ran special courses for Grenadian servicemen on how to use and maintain this equipment. Much later I met a Grenadian security guard who had been on one of these courses in the USSR, during his army service. He told me he wasn't interested in politics but the course was the only structured form of basic education he'd had in his life. I guess there were many naïve young men like that whose recruitment meant they had a positive role and were getting paid. I got the impression that he just felt he was doing something useful.

Anyway, when the Americans decided to go ahead with their intervention in Grenada on October 24 1983, they did not really know how much opposition they would meet on the ground. One of their first objectives was to 'rescue' two hundred students at the American Medical School, then based on a campus at Grand Anse beach, though it emerged later that they were not really in danger. Another objective was to rescue Sir Paul Scoon, Governor General of Grenada who, they said, was being kept under house arrest at his residence above St. George's. Their mission would be to evacuate him to the safety of the American flagship, the USS Guam laying off Grenada with the aircraft carrier, Independence. The US regarded Sir Paul as the only lawful authority in Grenada, being the only legitimate representative of the Queen.

A contingent of American Navy Special Forces, the Seals, was lowered into the grounds of the Governor's residence and overpowered a group of Grenadian soldiers guarding the place. But three Soviet armoured personnel carriers manned by Cuban crews, came into view and there was an exchange of fire. A Blackhawk armoured helicopter lowered more Seals into the grounds, but without heavy support they were trapped. The was grave concern about the inevitable diplomatic embarrassment, should Sir Paul be hurt or even killed in the action.

Five hundred airborne Rangers were parachuted onto the new airport at Point Salines which was heavily defended by Cuban soldiers and a firefight between them lasted some hours before the Americans secured the airfield. Two hundred Cubans surrendered, but over a hundred escaped. A group of American Marines then made a beach landing with the objective of helping the Seals still stranded at the Governor's residence. There was Cuban opposition on the way and it took them ten hours to get there. They were eventually successful though and evacuated the civilians, including the Governor. Ten Seals had been wounded before the action was over.

On Grand Anse, the Marines and Rangers evacuated the students off the beach by helicopter. It took several days to quieten pockets of resistance in various parts of the island before Grenada could attempt to settle down and lick its wounds. By the end of the intervention eighteen Americans were dead, with one hundred and sixteen wounded. Twenty-four Cubans and forty-five Grenadians had been killed, but twenty-one of those Grenadians were mental patients, who died when American pilots mistakenly bombed the mental hospital in St. George's.

There were also reports that some of the American troops drowned when they jumped off a landing craft too soon wearing full packs. What they thought was shallow clear blue water was probably twenty feet deep. Another report has an American soldier who got lost in the fray making a reverse charge call

183

from a public phone box to Fort Lauderdale in US and asking if they had any idea where his unit was: but everyone in Grenada has his own war story.

The documentation left behind by the People's Revolutionary Government apparently showed that the so-called 'leftist' faction was dedicated to turning the island into a Communist state. Maurice Bishop, a man with a genuine moral sense and a desire to help his people, had allowed himself to be manipulated by unscrupulous hardliners.

After the intervention the Deputy Prime Minister Bernard Coard, his wife and fifteen others were given death sentences for murder, later commuted to life imprisonment. Bernard Coard was released after twenty-six years and now lives in Jamaica. After his release he merely said: 'I think what is important is that we learn from the mistakes of the past.'

The University of St. George's Medical School, which includes a veterinary college, now has around six thousand students, mostly American and occupies a vast, state-of-the-art campus overlooking the sea. It accounts for about one third of the country's economy, the capitalist's dream. For teaching academics and students alike it's a perfect location looking out on to amazing Caribbean sunsets. No wonder those who work there cherish their jobs.

The University operates its own bus service for students and people working there, available day and night. One of their favourite haunts is a restaurant and music venue called Umbrellas, in a prime location on the beach at Grand Anse. It is full any night of the week ... a goldmine for the Grenadian family which runs it. Many years ago when they were looking for the best location to build their restaurant that particular spot was occupied by a little old lady who sold her goods from beneath a large umbrella. She persistently refused to sell the family her licence to be there ... until they gave her the best deal she could ever have wished for: they made her a partner and called the new establishment 'Umbrellas'. These days her son delivers meals to well-heeled students ... in his Mercedes.

CHAPTER 31

DRUMS AND COLOURS

My father-in-law, Stephen Scott, thought I was in danger of being possessed by the devil. He was a serious Catholic, probably on first name terms with a few cardinals in the Vatican, maybe even the Pope. But he was concerned that I had embedded myself in the African-rooted religion of Orisha, practised in Trinidad and Tobago since slavery, but much misunderstood and demonised over the generations. As far as he was concerned any faith influenced by cosmic forces was voodoo and to be avoided at all costs, but my involvement was purely journalistic research.

This week is Thanksgiving and I am in a rural garden at D'Abadie, near Arima, with an Orisha community which has existed for decades alongside Hindus and Muslims. The leader or high priestess of this Orisha parish is Mother Joan, an attractive, powerfully-built woman in her fifties who has patiently tried to introduce me to the way in which her religion works. There is nothing demonic about Orisha, nothing sinister. It is a non-Christian religion but, as with other belief systems, there is the notion of one supreme God...Oludumare.

Orisha spirits, many of them equated with Christian saints, are messengers between humankind and his divine kingdom. Shango, is the Yoruba god of fire, thunder and lightning. His wife, Oya, is mistress of speed and tempestuous wind and is paired with St. Catherine: Oshun, goddess of water and beauty is paired with St. Philomena: Osain Yoruba god of herbal medicine, healing and prophecy, with St. Francis: Shakpana, also a healer, especially of children's illnesses, with St. Jerome: Ogun, the warrior god of iron and steel, with St. Michael. Among the general public in Trinidad one may hear the name Shango being used to describe an entire belief system, when in fact Shango is only one of dozens of deities within the Orisha religion. Each one of these powers is attributed his or her own characteristics, likes or dislikes including favourite colours, which are taken into account when offerings are made during

Thanksgiving. During spirit possession, worshippers will take on some of these characteristics which have the effect of distorting their entire persona.

Historically, Orisha worshippers have shown a preference for aspects of the Catholic faith, though the dogma of the Church is virtually ignored. In the early 19th century, west African slaves in Trinidad were sometimes baptised into Catholicism en masse; it seems likely that many Orishas used the paraphernalia of the catholic church as camouflage behind which they hid their African beliefs from their masters. These African practises were demonised by plantation owners as obeah or witchcraft, with brutal consequences, if caught. Hence the need for secrecy. In modern times the Orisha religion has broadened its appeal in Trinidad. Participants were traditionally working class, but now there are professional middle-class followers, who have come to the faith as an act of political and ideological self-expression, a way of reclaiming their identity within the cultural mixture that is Trinidad today.

As I see it, the grassroots devotee derives a sense of well-being and self-worth from practising a religion which is essentially community-based and in such close touch with nature. The gods, or saints, are there to help the faithful cope with the stresses and strains of life, to protect the water, the soil, their food and even their roadways. Since there is no written liturgy in the Orisha faith, no sacred book, the continuity and uniformity of the religion depends on oral traditions maintained over the generations.

What struck me while I was with the Orishas in D'Abadie was that they not only knew each other very well, being a small community, but they genuinely cared for each other's well-being and went out of their way to help one another. The structure of each group and the shrine at which they worship is basically the same, as are the various objects or symbols inside the open-sided building where the singing, dancing and distinctive drumming takes place. Candles are lit at the four corners, where sweet olive oil or water will be poured from time to time as offerings to the gods. At one end of the room in front of three drummers, Ogun's sword is embedded in the earthen floor beside double-edged wooden axe and a shepherd's crook. Around the blade are candles, olive oil, water and rum. Dotted about the room, or chapelle, as it is called are statues or lithographs of Catholic saints.

Outside the shrine, in a corner of the garden, a number of flags fly on high bamboo poles, the likes of which can also be found in Hindu communities. The colours can change daily; they represent those gods expected to 'enter' on any particular night. Worshippers consider the flags as a conduit through which the spirits can enter the shrine. It is here, near the flags, that the slaying of any sacrificial animal takes place. Candles and stools are also placed at various points for the convenience of powerful deities and there is always a water trough or pond, many of their spirits being water gods. It seems that spirits, like people, demand a lot of attention and respect.

Tonight a red flag flies for Shango. It is nearing the moment for this Yoruba god of thunder and lightning to reveal himself through one of the worshippers, though no-one knows who that might be. They assume it will be one of the people within the shrine itself because outside the rain is lashing down. An appropriate night for Shango. There is rolling thunder and the lightning turns the bending palms into magnesium strips. For hours the drums have been pounding in a call and response pattern.

A woman standing next to Rowena starts to tremble and shake as her eyes roll up into her head. Next to her a man to whom we had been speaking earlier is changing character, his head jerking about like a hen as he hops onto one leg. Mother Joan had placed us in the middle of the crowd for the experience and that it was. Soon everyone is swaying around us. No-one speaks. They are leaping and twirling, faces contorted, as the drums speak to the ancient gods of Africa; but we feel trapped in a roomful of chaos. I notice that Horace Ove, the Trinidadian photographer friend I brought with me, has wisely positioned himself outside and is discreetly picking off shots through an open window.

I remember Mother Joan advising us that, when people are in spirit possession, we should avoid making eye contact, as it might be misinterpreted; so we try to appear nonchalant.

The electrifying drama is heightened by the fireworks display put on by mother nature in the night sky above us. Shango is still expected to manifest himself among the dancers inside, but tonight is different. Nobody seems to notice that a middle-aged man, who had been talking with friends on a verandah outside

187

the shrine, is now flat on his back in the mud and rain, stretched out like a corpse. I had been talking to him a day or so ago, a quiet, avuncular man who had travelled to the shrine every night of these celebrations from his home in Port-of-Spain some twenty miles away. Here he is now, entrenched like a stranded cayman, but suddenly starting to move, feet first, in seemingly uncontrollable spasms. The sheer effort of moving forward, inch by inch, towards the candles flickering in the doorway of the shrine, seems almost too much for him judging by his twisted face. It is as though the Earth's magnetism is reluctant to let him go. He is like a prisoner trying to free himself from invisible shackles.

The manic throng inside become aware that the manifestation they are awaiting indoors is slowly emerging from the storm. A candle in the doorway shows the way and olive oil is poured along the route. As if lifting some enormous weight, the fellow heaves himself out of the quagmire and crashes awkwardly into the door frame, one leg twisted beneath him. The air

Orisha followers in the throes of spirit possession during a Thanksgiving at their shrine in Trinidad.

is filled with incense being offered to the four corners of the building, like a Catholic mass. The drums and chanting reach a crescendo; women in white make a way clear for the man being 'ridden' by the spirit. Gradually he stands and moves into the light as if dragging chains.

He is divested of the sharp-edged jewellery around his neck and of anything else that might cause injury to himself or anyone else and his trousers are rolled up to his knees. Finally, as he tries to hold his balance, he is tied around the waist and shoulder with a length of red cloth. Then he staggers through the worshippers and into the chapelle which is said to be his earthly domain. In a matter of minutes he re-emerges, straight as a ramrod, now clutching the shepherd's crook.

Shango surveys his flock, like a concerned father making sure all is well. The drums are rolling quietly now. Mother Joan brings in a candle-lit dish containing sweet olive oil and a sacred thunder stone, said to be from Mount St. Benedict. She stands before Shango as devotees come in turn to kneel and receive his blessings. It is a powerful scene in which there is obvious respect for the shepherd in their midst, who is guiding their every move.

Shango himself is not without guardians. His wife, Oya, manifests herself in one of the white-robed ladies who is twirling around the floor brandishing an axe, as if to ward off unwanted spirits or visitors. She is a human tempest, one second in the centre of the floor and the next spinning outside into the storm to check the compound for anything amiss. She stops, axe in one hand, in front of people standing in the garden. She gestures that she wants them inside the shrine and her face also carries that simple message. One woman runs off into the night, shrieking.

The blessings, the chanting, the singing and drumming go on until a cock crow signals the thin light of dawn. Only then does the torrential rain stop and worshippers begin to step out into the warm promise of sunshine. Everyone is smiling and you'd think they were just arriving, fresh as paint, for a garden party. Several men, who had walked barefoot on burning coals at the height of spirit possession, appear unmarked and unperturbed. No-one seems to remember what they were like in spirit possession.

It had been the same all week, a gathering of some sixty or more people, young and elderly, from far and near, who came to Mother Joan's shrine at about ten o'clock in the evening, each wearing a dress and head-tie of a different colour, to please the spirits. During this week of marathons, Wednesday was yellow for the god Osain, he who protects the forest, who can help people in distress, who can find jobs for them and food. He has another attribute I would like to have known about sooner, as a long-time sufferer with back pain. Osain is said to be a very good chiropractor.

Shango night had coincided with thunder and lightning. Osain's evening is dry and yet wet with moonlight, palms pointing silver fingers into the shrine. Typically the celebration begins with Christian prayers, the drums rolling quietly as the Hail Mary was said. Then all sound ceases briefly and when the drums start again they are speaking a different language and so

189

are the worshippers. Instantly we are in West Africa. The song leader guides us through the musical offerings to different gods. There are invitation songs, all sung in Yoruba, asking the Orishas or saints, to visit the shrine and possess one of the devotees. During the course of the week there will also be acceptance songs as an expression of gratitude after manifestations, also work songs sung while a spirit is attending to or consulting with someone. There are also pleasure songs to entertain the gods after they have completed their work.

Usually the song leader sings for the saints in a particular order, but since there is no written liturgy the order may differ from shrine to shrine. Generally the sequence starts with songs for Eshu, the gateman, opening the way to a spiritual experience, then Ogun the protector, followed by Osain, Shakpana, Emanje (St. Anne), Oshun and Erele equated with Jonah, not as a saint as more of a prophet, which I suppose is reasonable given his adventures with the whale. Osain, said to take care of children, is very popular at Mother Joan's shrine. She has had ten of her own. Tonight the chapelle is jumping with manifestations, at one point half a dozen at a time, and there is an explosion of colour.

One of Mother Joan's daughters glides gracefully towards the drummers with a live morrocoy perfectly balanced on her head, the top of its shell lit by four candles. The morrocoy is one of the favoured offerings to Osain. So is the pure white goat which is brought into the throng to be washed and anointed with oil. There it stands, blissfully unconcerned. Finally it is led to all four candle-lit corners with other live offerings: a pair of ducks, a pair of hens, a pair of chickens. A man picks up the goat and dances with it draped around his neck. Then, amid the song and dance of celebration and a puff of incense, a pair of hands holds aloft a baby, only one month old, while prayers are sung for Osain to bestow blessings upon the child.

The night's spiritual activity moves on relentlessly towards its finale in the moonlit garden. The drummers have re-assembled beneath the flags to welcome those bringing their animals to the sacrificial altar. Prayers are chanted and the first in line, the white goat, no longer chewing, finds himself being danced around again, this time on Mother Joan's shoulders. Rowena, not wanting to look at what was going to happen next, has moved to the back of the group. The white goat is stood before

190

a high priest in flowing robes, his cutlass raised high. It falls swiftly, cleanly and the sacrifice is complete. The headless carcass, to be cooked later, is tossed over the people in front, landing at Rowena's feet. The live offerings continue.

Osain is well served this night. In the days to come all the food, when prepared, will be given to the needy in the district. I should mention that not all the shrines sacrifice animals. Some prefer to offer fruit instead either on moral or financial grounds or perhaps a combination of both.

There are some seventy Orisha shrines in Trinidad, but invitations to visit any of them do not come easily, which is understandable. The Orisha religion is sometimes mis-interpreted even among those who profess religious tolerance and so devotees are cautious about outsiders. It is interesting that Mother Joan's shrine is next to a Hindu community, who fly different flags in their gardens for different spirits. Some of the Hindus happily come to the Orisha ceremonies and vice versa: religious tolerance. History is important to all religious communities, including the Orishas, which might explain the move in recent times towards greater Africanisation. A people without a history is like a tree without roots. However, among the census-takers of Trinidad, the Orisha religion seems to be invisible, lost in the country's multicultural rainbow.

CHAPTER 32

MONEY TALKS

Trinidadians are canny when it comes to money and so was film-maker Ismail Merchant. When he brought his team to the island from London, Bombay and New York to shoot an adaptation of V.S. Naipaul's novel, The Mystic Masseur, the locals didn't want to sell themselves cheap, while the big-time producer was determined to keep a tight grip on the purse-strings.

His budget for this movie was a mere $2.5 million, which would barely cover the bill for meals on some of Merchant-Ivory's more lavish films. There had been precious little preparation on the ground before shooting started. Against local advice, Merchant had chosen to arrive in the middle of the furore surrounding a general election. The country's predominantly Indian party, the United National Congress, had just scraped to a contentious election victory. Allegations of large-scale gerrymandering and fraud filled the newspapers while the prime minister, Basdeo Panda and President Robinson were engaged in a constitutional mud-slinging contest.

Robinson had refused to sign documents allowing Panday to appoint seven ministers who had lost their seats in the election. Panday had been presented with a libel suit for calling someone a 'pseudo-racist' and added further fuel to the fire by claiming that the twin-island state was being threatened by an impending coup.

It was a warning that a lot of people took seriously. In 1990 there had been a real coup attempt in which several people were killed near the parliament building, although in the present situation it was probably just a ruse by the prime minister. Having narrowly won the election he perhaps wanted to create a little tension so that he could be seen as a safe pair of hands. After all, Panday, a former union leader and actor of no mean repute, was not known as 'The Silver Fox' for nothing.

Ismail Merchant had to be a supreme optimist when he bounced into the prime minister's newly-refurbished office and asked if the film company could borrow it for a weekend ... free of charge. The grand building, Whitehall, is one of the so-called Magnificent Seven buildings overlooking the Savannah in Port-of-Spain. The film-maker's charm and wide smile, which he could turn on like a light bulb, must have helped, but the prime minister wanted the film to be a success and so gave his permission for the film to take over Government House, just for a couple of days.

Merchant pushed his luck by asking whether the government might like to invest in his film, with no luck, although he did manage to persuade a local industrialist to part with half a million dollars for the picture, in exchange for a credit as an executive producer.

It was a daunting task finding all the props for a film set in the 1940ies and 50ies. The local people were exhausted searching all over the country; but, as if my magic, all that was needed materialised in the nick of time. There was a 1937 Vauxhall in pristine condition for the film's hero, Ganesh, as well as a 1952 gold Rolls Bentley for the smart colonial dinner scene at Government House, the prime minister's office. There were ancient bicycles hired from even older men who had been peddling around the cane fields on them since the forties. There was even a collection of colonial currency discovered at the home of a Trinidadian numismatist.

Merchant had delegated his young nephew, Nayeem Hafizka, who was leading the production team, to seek out as many local contacts as he could, as quickly as possible. Nayeem was his uncle's clone: the same charming smile, softly spoken, employing the same tenacious approach to wheeling and dealing until he got a discount on everything... from meals in restaurants to rented property for himself, the cast and crew. However his smooth talking didn't wash with the national airline who were adamant they couldn't give discounts, even for film people.

As Merchant was trying to shoot the movie on a shoestring, chicken and rice were the order of the day on the set, with a slice of currant cake for dessert, although when the prime minister took a break from his various crises and popped in for lunch they treated him to shrimp.

Despite Nayeem's efforts the purse strings were pulled a little too tight. Om Puri, star of East Is East and City of Joy, who played the scheming village storekeeper Ramlogan in the film, was prone to backache. After a few days and nights working he was in need of a rest, but all he could find to lie on were some planks of wood. He said there were only six chairs to be shared between sixty people. There wasn't even a doctor or nurse on the set. On his first day off I arranged for him to be seen by a Trinidadian masseuse, Molly Hardy.

Actor James Fox who flew 4,000 miles from London on a Saturday to play a spiritual recluse in a single scene, found himself filming the next morning, still jet-lagged and flying back to England the following Tuesday. Merchant wasn't about to subsidise a leisurely break on a palm beach.

Masseuse Molly Hardy brings relief to Om Puri, star of the film The Mystic Masseur, who suffered with real-life back problems for much of the shoot.

His frugality was really put to the test as they were about to film a scene in Port-of-Spain. The crew had cordoned off a street to traffic. They had chosen as their location an old printing works with a hand press, just the sort of place used in the novel by its protagonist, Ramesh Ramsumair, mystic healer and writer of books.

Suddenly, as they were preparing for the first take, a commotion broke out in the street. A family sitting outside their house refused to budge until they had been properly compensated. They were offered fifteen local dollars. No chance. They wanted 1,500 local dollars (about £150) and insisted. No-one had warned them that the street would be closed for two days. The police were called but the family still refused to move. Sensing an opportunity a barber and a barkeeper decided to join in. Both complained that they would lose so much trade they wouldn't be able to pay the rent at the end of the week.

Meanwhile the family, now squatting on the pavement, were warming to the idea of negotiation. If three of them were to be taken on as extras, they said, they might reconsider. For the first time, Merchant and his nephew lost their smiles and capitulated.

Finally filming got under way.

Opportunism was not the only problem facing the crew. Trinidad had little in the way of film infrastructure, no storehouse of historic treasures saved for posterity. The two English women responsible for set design and dressing became exhausted trying to find things in a hurry and a local producer, who'd been hunting around the island for suitable locations, quit the film in exasperation over the terms of her contract. She said so much was expected of her so quickly with so little reward that she felt she was being exploited.

Ismail Merchant was beset with money problems when he brought his production team to Trinidad to film an adaptation of V.S. Naipaul's novel The Mystic Masseur.

For the Indians who Merchant had flown from Bombay to help create his sets and attend to a hundred and one other manual duties, there was little relief. There they were in a foreign country, unsure of exactly where it was, with little time, little money and understanding nothing of the language. Yet they slogged diligently through their busy days with a smile. Everyone was impressed by the patience and good humour of Abdel the tailor who normally lived with his family in Bombay's Cardboard City. During the filming he lived in a room at the top of a house rented as an administrative base. There he worked on no less than 1,200 items of clothing for the film. Occasionally he would walk down the road to McDonalds where he could only afford the kid's menu. He kept the little toys that came with it for his children back home. For me, he was one of the silent heroes of the film.

The organisation of many film sequences was left to the very

195

last minute. When the producer needed a rain scene he asked for fire brigade help only the night before filming. In the Governor's ball scene someone had forgotten to hire a string quartet.

The Mystic Masseur was Merchant's fourth film as director. James Ivory had taken the helm on most of their previous collaborations … but it was his first film in Trinidad and he was having to learn the peculiarities of the island by trial and error.

Trinidad actors Michael Cherrie and Maureen Thompson wear what they think are appropriate clothes for guests invited to the governor's grand dinner and stick out like a sore thumb.

He had arrived in the country with the impression that the Pulitzer prize-winning author Naipaul must be a national hero and that local people would be only too happy to cooperate. He quickly discovered that the relationship between the author and his countrymen was something of a love-hate affair. Naipaul's fiction captured every twist and turn in the Trinidadian psyche and many did not appreciate his candour.

Some locals, however, were more sympathetic and willing to play a part in the movie as extras for 100 Trinidad dollars a day, about £10, although they might not have been so keen if they had known what they were undertaking.

In the scene set at the Governor's Ball some sixty Trinidadians were hired as extras. They arrived on the Saturday evening full of enthusiasm, chattering excitedly as they dressed for the shoot. Pretty soon they discovered what being an extra really entails: endless, agonising hours waiting for something to happen. That first attempt at filming was catastrophic. Not only had someone omitted to hire the musicians, the lighting was all wrong and the choreography just wasn't coming together.

196

Rowena and I were among the extras and at two in the morning, after standing around for so many hours, we were told to come back on Sunday afternoon because they were going to abandon the set for the night.

Come Sunday there were more hours of waiting for the extras, as the Governor's long and elegant table was properly laid for dinner to the producer's liking: resplendent with cut glass and silver. Some of those at the colonial bash came from old Trinidad plantation families, like Rowena, whose grandparents would have attended such grand affairs in the past. Some extras were countryfolk, like Ganesh the film's hero. They had not a clue about dress codes or the correct settings for the parade of different wine glasses, glinting at them from the crisp snow-white linen table-cloth.

Caryl Phillips, born in St. Kitts but brought up in Leeds, wrote the script for the film. One or two black Trinidadians were portrayed in the dinner scene, but as caricatures, while the behaviour of the Indian characters was equally understated. The two local black actors, Michael Cherrie and Maureen Thompson, playing invited guests, stood out like a sore thumbs. Michael wore a bright yellow suit and his companion, in billowing voile and bright headscarf, was straight off the top of a Christmas tree. Phillips managed to persuade the film editor to take out some of the more buffoonish stuff. His view was that the film had to portray race and class in the context of the period, with the film remaining true to the difficulties of that time.

CHAPTER 33

LIVING IN THE SOLUTION

As I had indicated in the early part of this book, when I was in Fleet Street I was very wary about drinking too much, because I could see what alcohol had done to some of my older colleagues. In those days the news-editor held his first planning meeting of the day in the bar of the pub next door. Every newspaper in Fleet Street had its favourite watering hole, some very appropriately named: the Daily Mirror's pub was The Stab in the Back.

There was the same drinking culture at the time among journalists in the BBC, though the amount of time they could spend at the bar was conditioned by their involvement in putting news programmes together.

Although I didn't understand it at the time, alcoholism is one of those diseases that makes you believe you haven't got it. Whenever I drank too much it was always easier to blame my habit on some situation or occurrence, bad or good. I could be drinking to celebrate something, or to console somebody or myself. To me, drinking too much seemed to be the norm among journalists. I didn't understand very much about the nature of alcoholism. It was just something that hadn't happened to me…yet.

I had no idea about the dangers of blackout: that point in drinking beyond which you have no memory, even though you appear to be functioning normally. The day after a drinking session, people would remind me of what I had said and done and I wouldn't be able to recall any of it.

At one time I volunteered to drive some elderly people, some disabled, to a bingo hall. Beforehand I was given a quick course in how to load their wheelchairs into a special bus.

On the night, I parked my car near the community centre and drove the bus to collect each one of them from their homes and deliver them to bingo. That was early in the evening. I was to come back for them at 10pm. No problem so far. But instead of playing it safe and going home for my supper I went into a pub. I had every intention of ordering a sandwich and a soft drink, but something compelled me to risk one scotch. It's true what they say about alcoholics – one drink is too much and a hundred drinks is not enough. I should have known that. I had no recollection of leaving the pub, collecting the bingo people, loading their chairs into the bus and taking them home. I didn't even remember where I parked my own car or the bus.

The next morning, I sat at home, waiting for a knock at the door, someone, maybe the police, calling to tell me of some disaster, but nothing happened.

I took a walk through the village to see if any of the people I had driven to bingo were around. I could see no one. I might have dropped them over a cliff into the sea for all I could remember. I was really ashamed that I had done something so dangerous. Eventually I rang the man who had trusted me with the job of driving the bingo people and asked him if I could pop the key to the bus through his letterbox.

He said "I think that would be a bloody good idea."

I tried to imagine what it must have been like for those people who had endured the journey home and I was horrified. I vowed I would never drink again, but then, I had done that so many times before.

Another time, when everyone was asleep, I collected all the empty scotch bottles I had hidden in an outhouse and threw them into the sea at high tide. We lived right on the water in a little West Sussex village. Having got rid of the evidence, I retired to bed. The next morning was terrible. The incoming tide had washed all the bottles back in and they littered the High Street leaving a trail…right to my door.

Sheepishly, I collected them all in a wheelbarrow, where everyone could see the culprit. Because I never knew what I had said and done in blackout I always imagined the worst and that probably, by now, the whole village was talking about me.

My sister Hillary died in 1992 from cancer at the young age of 54. She had said to me "Here I am, trying to hang onto life and there you are pissing it away." I felt so upset and guilty but I carried on drinking.

My father, who had been a lifelong smoker, died the following year aged 86 and though I was with him through his last difficult days, his death still didn't stop me drinking. My mother then died in 1996, aged ninety-two. I sat with her in hospital for days until she slipped away. I was continuing to drink, but I knew that somehow I had to seek help.

It had taken me so long to reach the point where I was really ready to stop drinking. Before that I had been in denial, convinced that I could do it alone, but my efforts always ended in failure. I lost a great deal of self-esteem and I felt empty, as though my own spirit had abandoned me. I was desperate and asked help from the area health authority. After a long assessment they found me a place at Clouds House, a rehabilitation centre out in the country, near Salisbury, in Wiltshire. All the counsellors there were themselves recovering alcoholics or addicts and they helped me to turn my life around.

From the moment I entered Clouds House that awful urge to have a drink mysteriously disappeared. Throughout this difficult time, Rowena stuck with me and kept us together. She was surprised that the regime at Clouds House was so strict, but it had to be in order to bring groups of addictive personalities to the point of surrender, from which they might begin their recovery. They told us that roughly one third of us would make it; one third would leave the programme because they couldn't take it, or be kicked out for some infringement of the rules and perhaps be re-admitted at some future date; the remaining one third of us would die. Chilling statistics.

I came to believe that only some spiritual force could help me recover and that I was completely powerless to achieve sobriety on my own. I accepted that with the Lord's guidance, the miracle of recovery could be gifted to me. It took me a year, with a sponsor, to work through the twelve-step programme of Alcoholics Anonymous and I have to say, that the ensuing freedom from the shackles of addiction, is absolutely priceless.

The world is a different place and I am grateful still to be alive and able to spend some of the time that remains for me, painting the best of it as an artist.

CHAPTER 34

A FATEFUL BLOW

Whenever anyone hears that we lived in the Caribbean after I retired from the BBC, they want to know why on earth I chose to return to the UK. There are two reasons. First, if Claire and Christopher were go to university in the country of their birth they needed to take up residence and sit their A Level exams. The second reason was that my soul is in England. It's where I have my roots and I where I have a strong sense of belonging. Wherever I had been on my travels, as soon as I flew over Lands End on the homeward stretch to Heathrow, the green patchwork quilt of southern England always remained a comforting sight.

We lived in Southsea while Christopher was at Portsmouth Grammar School and Claire was at the Girls' High School. Rowena took a three-year BA degree course in Art History at Sussex University, two hours drive, so to ease the pressure we stayed a few nights a week with her old schoolfriend, Catherine Gillo, in Brighton. Rowena was a dedicated student and we were all so proud to see her receive her degree at The Dome in Brighton, from Sir Richard Attenborough, the university's Chancellor.

With all this studying going on, I took up painting. I enrolled in evening classes where a whole new world of colour opened up. For the first time I really saw the English countryside's rich mosaic of greens, yellow ochres, burnt umber, cadmium yellows and reds. The seasonal changes were suddenly inspirational and I found that while trying to capture the reality on canvas, everything else happening in life was far from my mind. I could lose myself and become totally absorbed for hours. That's the way it's been since I first picked up the brushes. Every canvas is a challenge and though I have had some of my work in small, local exhibitions, I rarely think that the finished product is good enough to be displayed. I plod on, because when I really feel that I have got it right, it's a wonderful thrill.

Once Claire and Christopher had gone to university, Rowena and I bought a smaller house, a Victorian brick and flint terrace with a pretty garden, just a short walk from the centre of Chichester. It was Rowena's choice and a wise one because we were able to modernise and build a studio overlooking the garden, where I could retreat to paint. For seven years we enjoyed the best of two worlds: the history and charm of a town that predates the Romans and has a beautiful cathedral, while for the winter we flew to the warmth of the Caribbean. Early January would see us on our way to Grenada, to the same pool-side apartment just a stroll away through lush tropical gardens to the beach at L'Anse-aux-Epines.

One of Rowena's great pleasures was to explore the wilds of the forest with the Grenada Hash Harriers, a walking club, definitely not for the faint-hearted; she would sometimes return at sunset covered in mud, but with a big smile on her face. She was very fit and strong, so in 2016 when she was diagnosed with cancer of the colon, we thought that with quick treatment she would overcome the problem. Throughout her radiotherapy and chemotherapy she remained positive and managed to keep smiling despite the extreme pain. It was a terrible time and just when we thought the tumour was shrinking it metastasised into her lung.

Over one weekend her life started to slip away and her surgeon told us there was nothing more that could be done. We had gone from hope to hopelessness so fast, that I found it difficult to believe. Rowena managed somehow to cling to life for over a week, giving her brother Nigel and her sister Celia and all her old school friends a chance to visit her in hospital. She took strength from her Catholic faith and gave us all a tough lesson in how to die with dignity, passing away in her sleep on 23rd January, 2019. The Roman Catholic Cathedral in Chichester was already packed by nine in the morning for her Requiem Mass, which was organised by her brother and sister. Rowena meant a great deal to so many people from all over the world.

Now, for all of us, the slow process of healing from the loss had to be endured, as we started to learn how to live with the gaping void left in our lives. The first year was an emotional roller coaster with so many unanswerable questions: why did it happen to someone so young? Wasn't she supposed to live to a ripe old age? Did we do enough to help her?

I lived my life a day at a time, sometimes just hours at a time, as I learned that the process of grieving has to be slowly worked.

It will not be cheated and it will take as much time as is needed. It is not something that can be by-passed with a stiff upper lip. Our family world had changed for ever and bit by bit we had to start to accept the new order of life, even though it was so hard not to sometimes wallow in self-pity and fear. I seemed to be on the edge of tears all the time and would inwardly beat myself up for being so pathetic. Claire and Christopher were truly amazing in the way they dealt with their bereavement and in helping me cope: all three of us would shed our tears together without embarrassment, when the grief was too much, greatly helping me share the emotional distress.

I was lucky to have met the Reverend James Cooper, the chaplain at St. Wilfrid's Hospice in Chichester. Rowena would have entered his refuge, had she not passed away in hospital. For months James patiently guided me through the grief; from darkness into the light, for which I shall always be grateful. He helped me let go and move away from being captive to my grief.

Every day I cherish the many happy years Rowena and I shared together. I feel strongly that she is always with me in spirit, encouraging me to finish this memoir, while time is still on my side. I offer a few lines of comfort taken from a prayer said at the funeral of Rowena's mother, Freda:–

You mustn't tie yourself to me with tears
Be happy that we had so many years,
I gave you my love,
You can only guess how much you gave to me in happiness.
I thank you for the love you have shown
But now it's time I travelled on alone.

CHAPTER 35

BRIGHTER HORIZONS

It is now two years since Rowena's passing. Christopher and I returned to Grenada for a short visit at the beginning of 2020, before Covid 19 hit the world. The trip brought back all the happy family times we had spent there over the years. Rowena's sister Celia came over from Trinidad to join us for a few days and all was well with the world. There were moments when walking along Grand Anse beach or swimming alone in the warm sea I would feel an emptiness creep over me and a yearning for the unconditional love I had lost. There was another blow to the family in September when Rowena's brother Nigel also died from cancer, leaving his widow, Minnie, and his sister, Celia, to begin the grieving process all over again.

Over the past six months, while writing this memoir during the Corona Virus pandemic, I have often thought how fortunate I am to have the loving support of my family and a few faithful friends. It's enriching for me to hear my four grown-up sons and daughters talk so passionately about the paths they have chosen in life.

Jane is teaching special needs children and winning "outstanding" praise from Ofsted. Claire is a life coach with her own special way of handling difficult teenagers. Christopher, a man of many talents, is pursuing his passion for music. He is always 'on my case' in so far as my well-being is concerned. John, my oldest son, is something of a legend in the field of Chinese Traditional Medicine and Acupuncture. He and Jane live in Hastings, near their mother Gerry who, lives in Bexhill-on-Sea, where she spends most her time gardening and providing salad crops for everyone. From John's practice, The Yuan Clinic in south-west London, he keeps us all on track with his potions for good health.

I am so proud of them all and also of my seven grandchildren.

CHAPTER 36

A GOOD LISTENER

When I decided to write this book at the beginning of the first Covid lockdown of 2020, I was fortunate to have had a patient listener. Penelope Langhorne, one of my closest friends, loves to hear a good story and each day we would take a walk and I would talk about what I was going write later on in the afternoon.

Our walk was always the same come rain or shine: uphill for the first half, to challenge our limbs and then a downward slope homeward through grassy parkland. As the scenery around us changed through the seasons, we would take pleasure in the tiny details nature offered, to see us through the monotony of lockdown. There were also stories which I told her as I trawled through my memory bank. We might be forging our way up the track that runs above College Lane towards the university in Chichester, but in our imaginations we were far, far away, in equatorial Africa maybe or along the banks of the River Congo. No imminent danger lurking on our walk of course, no crocodiles or leopards, just cheeky squadrons of squirrels flirting in and out of the cow parsley around our feet.

"Let's take the first bit of the hill before you begin today's story," Penelope would say. It turned out that she was a steadier walker than I. You wouldn't believe that just over five years ago she suffered a stroke that half paralysed her, making it impossible to put one foot in front of the other. Here she was on our walk today, striding ahead of me, steady as a rock. She reached our first stop for a 'breather' and leant on some green railings, waiting for me to catch up. She always said that it was a miracle she survived her stroke. I maintained it was dogged determination.

The halfway mark on our walk was the wall at the entrance to the college, where we stopped for another little rest. This is where the stories picked up their pace as the going got easier. We crossed the road and at the entrance to Oaklands Park we would check the tops of two bollards for the ladybirds that seemed to be always there, hunting for minute insects. A few yards beyond our walk led to a communal vegetable garden, bursting with rhubarb, spinach lettuce and leeks.

Our walk then opened onto the downward slope of Oaklands Park playing fields where, at the bottom, between the rear of the Festival Theatre and the archery club, there was the greatest find of all...the communal orchard, with some of the rarest varieties of apple: the Salcote Pippin, the Egremont Russet, first introduced locally in the 19th century, together with all manner of plums. We would stand in the lush long grass beneath the trees while I finished telling my story for the day and then enjoy our favourite fruit of all, the really succulent greengages.

Two seasons have now passed in these green pastures and my storytelling has come to an end with my book hopefully moving closer to the publisher. Sadly Penelope has been stricken once again, this time with cancer and our walks are on 'hold'. Whatever the medics may say, Penelope has always believed in miracles!

BIBLIOGRAPHY

Martin Bell: *War and Peacekeeping* (One World Publishing 2020)

Ronnie Biggs and Chris Packard: *Odd Man Out – The Last Straw* (MPress 2011)

Tim Butcher: *Blood River* (Vintage Books 2008)

John Mendes: *Côté ci Côté la – The Trinidad & Tobago Dictionary* (Zenith, Trinidad 2012)

George Eaton Simpson: *Religious Cults of the Caribbean* (Industrias Graficas, Spain 1970)

Gregory Sandford and Richard Vigilante: *Grenada: The Untold Story* (Madison Books 1984)

David Tindall and Derek Humphry: *False Messiah* (Hart-Davis MacGibbon 1977)

Susan Travers and Wendy Holden: *Tomorrow to be Brave* (The Free Press 2001)

ACKNOWLEDGEMENTS

Many thanks to my family and friends who have supported me through the writing of this book, especially my neighbours Angela and Richard Saffery, Michelle and Ben Diplock, Dan Shaw and Mandy O'Flynn who came to my rescue when my computer skills failed me.

My gratitude also goes to my dear friend Miranda Bell for her unswerving confidence in me and to my editors Mark Vere Nicholl and John Owen Smith for their patience and guidance through the work.

Printed in Great Britain
by Amazon

69354765R00119